EVIDENCE
IN CAMERA

To those
who encouraged me to
write this book

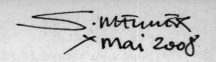

EVIDENCE
IN CAMERA

THE STORY OF PHOTOGRAPHIC
INTELLIGENCE IN THE
SECOND WORLD WAR

CONSTANCE BABINGTON SMITH

SUTTON PUBLISHING

This book was first published in 1957 by
Chatto & Windus

This new edition first published in 2004 by
Sutton Publishing Limited · Phoenix Mill
Thrupp · Stroud · Gloucestershire · GL5 2BU

British Library Cataloguing in Publication Data
A catalogue record for this book is available from the
British Library

ISBN 0 7509 3648 7

Typeset in 11/13pt Photina.
Typesetting and origination by
Sutton Publishing Limited.
Printed and bound in Great Britain by
J.H. Haynes & Co. Ltd, Sparkford.

CONTENTS

FOREWORD

by
Marshal of the Royal Air Force
The Lord Tedder G.C.B.

Photographic reconnaissance was not a new technique born in 1939. Twenty-two years before the second war broke out No. 70 Squadron R.F.C., in the course of three days, lost all three Flight Commanders and all its most experienced crews while attempting to carry out long-range (by current standards) photographic reconnaissance for GHQ. Not one aircraft of the final sortie of six returned. A few days later the job was taken over by the new DH 4 which had the performance (speed, height, and range) allowing it to operate singly and almost unchallenged as did the Mosquitos twenty-five years later.

The availability and suitability of the DH 4 for PR work was largely fortuitous and this may have led the Staffs before 1939 to assume that current types of bomber aircraft would be able to carry out this work – if indeed anyone had even dreamed of the ultimate scope and scale of photographic reconnaissance. Be that as it may, the sad result was that, just as in 1917 the Sopwith two-seaters of 70 Squadron were sacrificed attempting an almost impossible task, so from 1939–41 the Blenheims had to continue the struggle for PR until, despite the urgent and insatiable demands of Fighter defence, sufficient Spitfires had been made available, modified, and developed for this highly specialized task.

If ever the need arises again it is to be hoped that events will prove that we have been wise before the event.

The story of the development and achievements of the twin arts of photographic reconnaissance and photographic interpretation, so brilliantly told in this book, is to me the most fascinating aspect of the last war; a story of British genius at its best, the genius which can weld into a perfect team a wide variety of highly individualistic individuals, and harness to the common cause their widely differing temperaments and skills while allowing full scope for their individual originality, enthusiasm, and initiative. It is a story of imagination, devotion, and courage whose contribution to the ultimate success of the Allied cause was quite incalculable.

PREFACE

Many of us who were in Allied Photographic Intelligence in the Second World War hoped that in time there would be a book to put on public record the outstanding achievements of the reconnaissance pilots and photographic interpreters, as well as the contribution of the many others who made their work possible. I never expected that I myself would be called upon to write such an account, but I am very glad that the opportunity came.

As far as possible I have checked all facts and dates with contemporary records. The Air Ministry kindly gave me permission to study relevant documents, including Interpretation Reports, and I would like to thank Mr J.C. Nerney and his staff at the Air Historical Branch, and also Squadron Leader T.W. Oakey, for their assistance in this matter. I am also indebted to Air Marshal Sir Geoffrey Tuttle, Deputy Chief of the Air Staff, for his personal interest in the book and his helpful advice. I am, in addition, very grateful to the US Air Force for its cooperation, particularly to Captain James F. Sunderman of the Office of Information Services, who arranged for certain documentary material to be made available to me.

The material for this book has been collected primarily by talking with scores of my former colleagues, both here and in America – men and women who actually took part in the events I describe. My gratitude to them is beyond words. The memories they have shared with me are the flesh and blood of the story. A number of them have also given me invaluable help by reading and criticizing my draft. My only regret is that in the space of this book I cannot pay tribute to more than a few of those whom I would have liked to mention by name.

C.B.S.
Cambridge
July 1957

ONE
FASTER AND HIGHER

'The photographs showed . . .' In almost every account of the Second World War, whether from the viewpoint of Air Force, Navy, or Army, these words recur again and again. For during the last war the searching eye of the aerial camera became, to the Allies, much more than an important tactical adjunct to military operations, which had previously been its accepted wartime role. During the years between 1939 and 1945, a new kind of photographic reconnaissance, strategic as well as tactical, came into being, carried out first from Britain, and then from Allied bases all over the world. The intelligence it yielded gave answers of a rapidity, scope, and accuracy which had never before been envisaged.

Behind the words 'the photographs showed . . .' there is a story which is essentially twofold; for this new intelligence was the product of two extremely different activities: the taking of the pictures and the reading of their meaning. In the records of flying achievement, the photographic pilots have hitherto received little acclaim; but in many ways their work was even more demanding than that of the bomber and fighter pilots. For normally they flew alone and unarmed to their targets, and even after the photographs were taken, often from five miles up, the job was only half done: the sortie was wasted unless they got the pictures back safely.

Even when the pilot was back, however, his films meant nothing without the interpreters. Many of the

1

illustrations in this book may arouse the comment: 'I can see for myself what is of military interest without having to be called an interpreter'; and it is quite true that certain things of military interest can be recognized by anyone in certain pictures. But the vast majority of the war's aerial photographs were taken from great heights and from immediately above, and the wealth of information they hold has meaning only for the initiated. Indeed, their secret language may be compared to the language of X-ray photographs, which can be fully understood only by an eye which is experienced and a mind that has been specially trained.

The idea of taking photographs from the air is nearly as old – or as young – as aviation itself; and just a hundred years ago it began to inspire a number of aeronauts and photographers in several different countries. Earliest of them all was the famous French pioneer photographer Nadar (Felix Tournachon), who fixed a camera on the basket of a balloon and took the first successful aerial photographs near Paris in the spring of 1856. He followed this up by obtaining many excellent views of Paris, and those he got in 1858 received much publicity and are often alluded to as the first aerial photographs ever taken. But Nadar declined the opportunity to make yet more history. In 1859 he was invited by the French Minister for War to apply his experiments to the military field, but his politics restrained him and he evaded the proposal.

A year later, in 1860, a successful photograph of Boston was taken from a balloon by J.W. Black; and only two years after this, according to some historians, aerial photography was first used for a military purpose in the American Civil War. The story goes that in 1862 General McClellan, in command of the Northern Army besieging Richmond, Virginia, sent up a photographer in a tethered balloon to take a picture of the Confederate troops and batteries. Two prints were made, and each was marked off into sixty-four squares. General McClellan had one, and two balloonists took the other and ascended with it to 1,500 feet over the battlefield. From this point of vantage they telegraphed to the General the exact movements of the enemy troops on the numbered squares. It worked splendidly, and the Confederate attempts to break through the besieging lines were countered by reinforcements.

In England in 1863, Henry Negretti and James Glaisher took photographs successfully from free balloons at higher altitudes than Nadar, and from this time onwards there were many experiments, both in Europe and America, with cameras attached to balloons and some to kites and rockets. By the eighties, balloon units for reconnaissance were being started up on both sides of the Atlantic.

Photographs were first taken from actual aeroplanes in 1909, and again America and France led the way. On 24 April 1909, Wilbur Wright himself, accompanied by a photographer whose name is unrecorded, took off from Centocelle, near Rome, and succeeded in obtaining a series of cinematograph pictures. At about the same time French photographers started experimenting on similar lines, and the first effective stills were those taken by M. Meurisse in December of 1909. During the next five years the work of the pioneers continued apace, and the way was soon open for the successes of the First World War.

When August 1914 came, however, aerial reconnaissance was still primarily visual, and such were the first reconnaissance flights of the Royal Flying Corps, made on 19 August by Captain Joubert de la Ferté and Lieutenant G.W. Mapplebeck. But the idea of using the camera to supplement the human eye was already being pursued by both sides. At first the French were ahead in this field, but the British were soon following their lead and in due course Lieutenant J.T.C. Moore-Brabazon was put in charge of a small photographic unit. By March 1915 a trench map prepared chiefly from aerial photographs was used with great success by Sir Douglas Haig in the attack at Neuve Chapelle, and from then on there was a continual urgent demand for photographic reconnaissance, both for making maps and for checking enemy activity.

At the start of the war some of the Army diehards had felt it was unsporting to photograph the German rear positions, but these scruples were soon forgotten. By mid 1915 both sides were hard at it, and both sides were realizing that steps must be taken to prevent the enemy from recording their secrets from above. This need stimulated the rapid development of aircraft equipped with guns, for the work of the reconnaissance planes was so vital that they had to be protected – by an escort of specialized fighting aircraft.

Later in the war, photography also proved of decisive value in Egypt and Palestine; firstly for mapping, because in many areas the existing maps were no use. But one of the photographic officers of the RFC who took part in this work, Lieutenant Hugh Hamshaw Thomas, became much interested in studying the photographs further; and thus he gradually accumulated a fund of knowledge about what military installations look like from above. It was largely thanks to him that much invaluable data on the Turkish fortifications and batteries was available when General Allenby came to plan his attacks.

By 1918 photographic reconnaissance was being used to a lavish extent. There had been great advances in camera design and photographic techniques, as well as in the methods of deriving information from the pictures – methods which soon became known as photographic interpretation. A great revolution had taken place in the whole field of military intelligence. The traditional methods of obtaining information – the reports of secret agents, censors, and interrogators – were not superseded, but they were supplemented, in the same revolutionary manner that the traditional methods of communication had been supplemented by the telephone and wireless telegraphy. By the time of the Armistice, photographic intelligence had indeed proved itself, and was recognized on every hand as the indispensable eye of a modern army. But largely because of the technical limitations of the day – the performance and range of the aircraft and the scope of the cameras – it had come to be regarded as essentially of tactical value, and after the war this concept became frozen stiff in the thinking of the Staff Colleges of the world.

Such was the background when in 1938 it became clear to many that a second world war was inevitable. During the twenty years of peace there had been steady development in the civil applications of aerial photography; but the precedents of the First World War still dominated the military scene.

In Germany, where the vast expansion of the new Luftwaffe was forging ahead, much thought had been given to providing for photographic intelligence, particularly in relation to the needs of the Army. The whole matter was taken very seriously, and it is alleged that General von Fritsch, soon after he fell from Nazi favour and was dismissed from office as Commander-in-Chief of the German Army, went so far as to forecast that the side with the best photographic reconnaissance would win the next war. But his death in 1939 was to prevent him from seeing his prophecy fulfilled.

During the anxious years before war actually came a member of the Air Staff Intelligence named Frederick Winterbotham was a frequent visitor to Germany. He had a number of acquaintances in important positions, and this gave him chances to collect a lot of useful 'unofficial' information for Britain – up until September 1938. But after Munich, the Nazi and Fascist security systems were drastically tightened, and 'information' became much harder to get. In this predicament his mind turned back to his own experiences in the First World War, when as a Pilot in the Royal Flying Corps he had often escorted photographic aircraft and had first seen what valuable information aerial photographs could provide. Why not use the same method to help in keeping track of the German war preparations? It would, of course, have to be done very discreetly; in fact, it must be completely secret. He knew that his colleagues in the French Deuxième Bureau had already resorted to taking photographs from civil planes whenever opportunity offered. Soon he had evolved a plan and obtained the necessary approval to go ahead. The next thing was to find the right man for the job. It was indeed fortunate for the whole future of British photographic intelligence that just at this point Winterbotham was introduced to a remarkable Australian called Sidney Cotton.

If Frederick Sidney Cotton had lived a few centuries earlier, he would have made a splendid buccaneer. He loved adventure for adventure's sake, continually defied the orthodox, and had a notable record for getting what he wanted by hook or crook. He also had a flair for mechanical things, and was naturally inventive: in fact, one of his inventions had long since made his name a household word in aviation: during his time in the Royal Naval Air Service in the First World War he had invented the windproof 'Sidcot' flying-suit, forerunner of the one-piece 'siren suit'.

Between the wars he was busy with various flying ventures, and developed air mail services in Newfoundland, where he also tried his hand at aerial survey. Later he became interested in colour photography, and it was in this connexion that in the summer of 1938 he was back in England, establishing business contacts in Germany for his colour film company. Here was the right man for the scheme that Winterbotham envisaged.

Without delay the plan was finalized, and the project, which was to be strictly on a civilian footing, received the blessing of the Chief of the Air Staff, Air Chief Marshal Sir Cyril Newall. Then Winterbotham and Cotton could go right ahead, and between them they worked out the details. The success of the scheme would depend entirely upon evading detection, so the photography would have to be done from as high as practicable, and an aeroplane of good performance was needed. An opulent twin-engined aeroplane, a Lockheed 12A, was selected: the range and ceiling of this little airliner were just what was needed. Then in dramatic secrecy it was equipped with hidden cameras. Cotton designed a frame for three cameras in the bottom of the passenger cabin. The central camera was mounted to photograph directly downwards, and the other two – one on either side – were at an angle to take obliques; the three together thus covering a wide area. Each camera operated in a continuous sequence, so that the photographs would overlap, giving a view of long strips of country. And underneath the whole installation there was a sliding panel, fitted so perfectly that when closed it was more or less invisible. Finally, the Lockheed was painted an exquisite duck-egg green. It was nothing unusual to paint an apparently private aeroplane in some gay colour; but it was not by chance that Cotton chose a colour which would make his plane practically invisible from far below.

It was nothing unusual, either, for Sidney Cotton to start up a new venture in aviation, and early in 1939 it was arranged for a small company called Aeronautical Research and Sales to be formed, with offices in St James's Square. The activities of this company, combined with the colourfilm business, were going to mean an intensive programme of business trips, and provided an excellent excuse for a lot of flying. A young Canadian, Robert Niven, who had just reached the end of his short service commission in the RAF, was engaged to help with the Lockheed, and together Cotton and he went off from Heston airport, where the plane was kept – time and time again – to many of the capitals and industrial cities of Europe, but especially to Berlin.

So far so good; but although the innocent-looking civil aircraft flew happily on its travels, and at 20,000 feet or so passed unobtrusively over many interesting places, it was not a simple straightforward matter to take photographs from such heights, for the lenses of the cameras reacted to the extreme cold, and got badly frosted up. Cotton was not to be defeated however, and he worked out a way of directing on to the cameras the warm air from inside the aircraft, so that for the first time photographs could be reliably taken from high altitudes. After this hurdle had been surmounted, extra fuel tanks were fitted which gave the Lockheed a greatly extended range; and in the spring of 1939 Cotton and Niven went off on a long 'Mediterranean tour', flying direct to Malta from Heston, and took roll after roll of photographs over Libya, Eritrea, Sardinia, and the Dodecanese. While Cotton was at Malta, taking photographs of some of the Sicilian airfields, a fateful meeting took place; for stationed at Malta at the time was a young man called Flying Officer Maurice Longbottom, who was later to join forces with Cotton in developing photographic reconnaissance.

The Lockheed landed back at Heston with a great cargo of films, and this brought up in a critical form the question of how to get the information out of them. For although the art of interpreting air photographs had been developed quite a long way in the First World War, in the summer of 1939 there was precisely one experienced interpreter at the Air Ministry, Squadron Leader Walter Heath. Between the wars it had not been considered that the specialist interpreters would be needed, for interpretation was supposed to be a job that any Station Intelligence Officer could be trained for in a week or two, and Heath's job was organizing courses for them. For a time Heath struggled to keep up, and one or two Intelligence Officers helped as best they could, but there was inevitably a serious time-lag. It was not until much later in 1939, however, that another solution was found for this particular problem.

During the last months before war began there was still much private flying for pleasure as well as for business, and the international flying meetings were the great events of the summer season. On 28 July 1939, the first day of the special air rally put on by the Nazis at Frankfurt, the elegant duck-egg Lockheed circled in to land at the large new airport, and taxied up to join a motley crowd of little aircraft of all shapes and colours. In Cotton's party were Charles Grey, the Editor of *The Aeroplane*, and Margaret Gilruth, an Australian journalist.

The Berlin agent for Cotton's colour-film business, Herr Schöne, who had been in Richthofen's squadron with Goering in the First World War, was waiting to meet the party, and he introduced them to everybody, including some of the many Luftwaffe officers who were present, from General Milch downwards. Cotton recounts how the conversation invariably turned to the 'kolossal Lockheed'. Soon one of the Generals, who was chief of the Tempelhof airport at Berlin, made it clear that he would very much like to go up for a flight, and Cotton was delighted to oblige. On a sudden impulse he recalled that a favourite aunt of his had always raved about the beauty of the Rhine at Mannheim. He would love to fly the General over this beautiful region if it could be permitted. It *was* permitted; and the following day many more similar flights were permitted. In fact, there was quite a bit of competition for joyrides in the Lockheed. Accompanied by a series of Lufftwaffe generals and colonels, Cotton flew hither and thither at a couple of thousand feet, over the airfields and ammunition dumps, the factories and fortifications. And while his passengers commented with interest on the Lockheed's performance, Sidney casually flicked a little switch, and down below the camera went clicking away.

As day by day the summer of 1939 led towards war, Cotton's business trips to Germany became more frequent than ever. Each time he flew between London and Berlin he would take a slightly different route, and each time he saw with apprehension the swarms of fighters and bombers that were gathering at the various airfields. Fred Winterbotham's idea was producing some very interesting results.

About the middle of August, when Cotton landed at Tempelhof from London after taking a more northerly course than usual, the control officer asked to see him. 'Are you not flying from London on rather a roundabout course?' he asked. Cotton replied that he always flew on a great circle route, and the control officer tried hastily to conceal his ignorance. 'Oh, like Lindbergh,' he said. 'Thank you. I beg your pardon for having to ask you.'

But things did not always go as easily as that, and in the third week of August 1939, during the days of agonizing suspense after the pact between Germany and Russia had been announced, Cotton was actually in Berlin, and for a short time it looked as if he might be trapped there; for suddenly all civil flying was stopped. But finally he was given clearance, and he took off for England, with much trepidation, on 24 August. The Lockheed was to be allowed to fly to the Dutch frontier unchallenged by anti-aircraft guns, but if it strayed even slightly from its prearranged course it would be shot at.

Cotton's course took him near Wilhelmshaven, where he saw a great number of German ships. As he crossed the Dutch frontier, with a sigh of relief, he turned to look back, and the ships were silhouetted in the distance. They looked like little dark grey pencils, and with them there was a tiny white glimmer – Hitler's yacht *Grille*.

Eight days later Hitler invaded Poland. It could only be a matter of a day or two before Britain and Germany were at war. So it was suddenly of the utmost importance to the Admiralty to know for certain which ships were in Wilhelmshaven. Since war had not actually been declared, however, the RAF could not be asked to send out a reconnaissance plane, and instead the Admiralty appealed to Fred Winterbotham. He put it to Cotton, who said he would be delighted to try for photographs. Fresh in his mind was the memory of those distant silhouettes he had seen as he crossed the Dutch frontier, and it had actually occurred to him at the time that an oblique photograph of the great naval base could be taken from inside the Dutch frontier, if you were at the right height.

By this time a second aeroplane had been acquired, a little Beechcraft, and as Bob Niven was very keen too make the flight, Cotton agreed to let him go off in it, accompanied by a photographer who Winterbotham had brought along. From high above Gröningen the grey pencils at Wilhelmshaven were photographed, and Niven and his companion were soon back at Heston.

Cotton was on tenterhooks till the films were processed, but his eyes lit up when he saw the negatives. There were the ships, silhouetted in the distance. Some big enlargements, though they would be grainy, should enable the experts at the Admiralty to identify the individual units. He waited impatiently while the enlargements were made, and then tore off to Whitehall.

On the following day, when war was declared, and when the new First Lord of the Admiralty Winston Churchill picked up the reins again after almost twenty-five years' absence, the Director of Naval Intelligence was ready for questions on the whereabouts of the German fleet.

●　　●　　●

Less than an hour after the declaration of war, a Blenheim of Bomber Command took off from Wyton on the war's first official photographic sortie from Britain. Its purpose was to photograph the German Fleet at Wilhelmshaven, for Bomber Command was planning to stage an attack. The Blenheim pilot, Flying Officer A. McPherson, managed to bring back news that some of the ships were emerging from the naval base; and again when he went the next morning to re-check their position he succeeded in photographing the ships in the Schillig Roads.

But the raid which ensued brought shocking proof that the excellent Blenheim was not suitable for daylight bombing against heavily defended targets, and there were tragic losses. And in spite of McPherson's initial success, the fact that neither the Blenheim nor the current RAF cameras, as they were then being operated, were any use at all for reconnaissance under war conditions emerged mercilessly during the next few weeks. The Blenheims were an easy prey to both anti-aircraft guns and fighters, and except at dangerously low altitudes the cameras froze up, the films cracked, and the lenses frosted over.

The Air Staff was not slow to seek a remedy. On 15 September, Fred Winterbotham told Cotton that Air Vice-Marshal Richard Peck, the Director-General of Operations, would like to meet him to discuss the problems of aerial photography.

Next morning Cotton was at the Air Ministry, and Peck explained the trouble they were having with the RAF equipment. Cotton outlined his ideas, but they seemed too simple and were not accepted. The following day they met again, however, and this time the Deputy Chief of the Air Staff, Air Vice-Marshal Richard Peirse, joined the discussion and explained that there were two particular targets of which photographs were very urgently needed. The First Lord of the Admiralty, and indeed the Prime Minister himself, was most disturbed at the RAF's failure to photograph them during the previous ten days. Sidney remarked that if he could borrow a Blenheim he could get the photographs right away, but it was obvious at once that this offer would not be accepted. An RAF aeroplane could not be 'lent' to a civilian. But at the end of the morning it was agreed that the matter should be looked into further the following day, when an Air Force camera expert and some of the operation pilots would be called in.

Cotton left the Air Ministry and returned to his office

on the top floor of a building in St James's Square. He gazed out of the window, groping for a solution to the morning's problems. It was a lovely warm day, with big white clouds floating by. An idea suddenly came to him, and he phoned Bob Niven at Heston to ask for the weather report for Holland. Within a few minutes Niven called back to say the weather was good, and Cotton immediately told him to warm up the Lockheed ready for take-off. Next he telephoned to Fred Winterbotham and asked if he could arrange for some photographs to be processed later in the day, and then he hopped into his car and was at Heston half an hour later.

Winterbotham had arranged some time earlier that both the Lockheed and the Beechcraft should be allowed to fly anywhere with no questions asked, and the Heston control tower merely notified Fighter Command that the Lockheed was proceeding out to sea over Ramsgate for several hours on a test flight, and returning the same way. So there was no delay, and when the Lockheed was in the air Cotton told Niven what he had in mind. A mischievous grin spread across Niven's face as they climbed to the top level of the floating clouds, and dodging from one to another made swiftly for the Dutch coast. A couple of hours later they were back. Both of the targets had been photographed without any enemy interference at all.

By the next morning Cotton had an album full of magnificent enlargements, each with an overlay trace showing features of special importance. In Peck's office at ten o'clock the meeting assembled as planned, and after half an hour's talk Cotton mentioned that he had some samples with him, and he would like to know if these were the sort of pictures that were wanted. He produced the album, which was handed round and much admired. Everyone seemed to assume that the photographs had been taken somewhere before the war, and Peck remarked that they would not expect such good quality under war conditions. At last someone asked when they were taken.

'At three-fifteen yesterday.'

'What are these pictures?' demanded several voices at once.

'The places you wanted photographed,' said Cotton. There was a moment's astounded silence and then an explosion of protests, and before the commotion had subsided Cotton was out of the room.

That evening Peck phoned Fred Winterbotham and asked if he would be willing to hand over the 'Cotton outfit' to work for the RAF if they could find some way to fit it in. Winterbotham gladly agreed, and told Peck that in his view Cotton's technique of high-altitude photography ought to replace the existing Air Force methods.

So next day Cotton was asked to come to Peck's office at 12.30, and after a few minutes they were joined by the Chief of the Air Staff, Sir Cyril Newall.

'So *you* are the person who is giving us all this trouble,' said Newall.

'No, sir,' replied Cotton, 'his name is Hitler.'

Newall smiled. 'In spite of your unorthodox behaviour,' he said, 'I want to congratulate you on the pictures you produced yesterday. I'm glad to tell you they have served their purpose.' Then suddenly he asked, 'What's wrong with the Air Force's photography?'

'Do you really want the truth, sir? If so, you must remember that I'm an Australian, and someone once said that an Englishman calls a spade a spade but an Australian calls it a bloody shovel.'

Newall smiled again, and asked Cotton if he was free for lunch.

Over lunch at the United Service Club they discussed the reasons why the RAF photography had failed while Cotton's had succeeded. Cotton recalls that almost at once Newall asked him if he would be prepared to join the RAF and help to put right its existing photographic set-up.

'Not on your life,' replied Cotton. 'That wouldn't get results quickly enough.' He knew this was the moment to take the plunge, and he went on to suggest that if Newall would allow him to form a special unit, and give him *carte blanche* as to the choice of men, machines, and equipment, he would take the job on, provided he could do it as a civilian. 'It's the only way if you want results.'

Newall did not hesitate for a moment. He agreed to the idea on the spot, *carte blanche* and all, and asked Cotton if he had any suggestion as to where he should work from.

'What about Heston? No one will suspect that secret work would be done at a commercial airport.'

'Yes, you've got something there. Heston it is.'

Cotton could hardly believe it was all true, and thought perhaps the time had come to soft pedal a bit, so he assured Newall he would do his best to keep within the channels and routine of the Air Force. But the answer was an unexpected one.

'No, for God's sake don't do that, Cotton. Your value to me is that you will continue to do things in your own way. I want results.'

So a few days later, on 22 September 1939, the 'unofficial' partnership of Sidney Cotton and Fred Winterbotham was brought to an end, and Peck initiated Sidney into the mysteries of starting up a special secret unit within the RAF. At once it became apparent that there was no machinery by which Air Force planes and equipment could be handed over to a civilian, so Cotton reluctantly agreed to accept a commission, but only on condition that he had a free hand. He was thereupon commissioned as Squadron Leader, with acting rank of Wing Commander, and Bob Niven became a Flight Lieutenant, while as an additional pilot Cotton asked for Flying Officer Longbottom, whose intelligence and interest in photography had so much impressed him at Malta earlier in the year.

A Squadron Leader named Lionel Stubbs, whom Cotton later found to be exceptionally knowledgeable, was then brought in, and he helped Cotton to chart his course along the unfamiliar channels of RAF procedure. Stubbs told Cotton to name the people he wanted, and he would have them posted to the unit, which was to be known as the Heston Flight. Cotton cabled to America, to one of the top technicians in his colour-film company, Paul Lamboit, whom he wanted to run his photographic section; and Stubbs helped him to find other personnel, including a redheaded ex-policeman named Belcher as equipment officer. As regards accommodation, the Flight took over one of the Heston hangars, and also the flying club premises and part of the Airport Hotel.

All the various administrative wheels were now beginning to turn, at the Air Ministry and at Fighter Command, to which the Heston Flight was attached. It was Stubb's idea that the unit should be administered by Fighter Command, on the grounds that as they would not be a 'client' for photographs they would probably not interfere.

Cotton's most serious worry was about suitable aircraft. He already knew exactly what he wanted for the job ahead of him, and his ideas were more than ambitious: he wanted the aircraft which was the fastest fighter in the world – the RAF's precious new Supermarine Spitfire. Speed and altitude ahead of everything else in the sky would be the essence of the new technique he envisaged. The time was ripe for aerial reconnaissance of quite a new order, and it was providential that this realization came to Sidney Cotton as well as to a few others who were less well equipped to bring it to consummation. There is a saying that although Icarus and Leonardo da Vinci thought of flying, it took the Wright brothers to put it across.

In 1939 the Air Ministry's department concerned with the supply of aircraft had been evacuated to Harrogate, so Cotton went off there at once with what he thought was a simple request for a couple of Spitfires. The Chief of the Air Staff had given him *carte blanche* as to men, machines, and equipment, so he did not expect any difficulty. But he still had a lot to learn about the Royal Air Force.

He was ushered into the office of Air Vice-Marshal Tedder, and full of enthusiasm he presented his case. The 'eyes' of the three Services were going to play one of the most important roles in the war, he explained with animation. Photographic intelligence must be built up on lines which would give full freedom of action and at the same time limit losses to a minimum. The new unit must always get its pictures back to base. If the aeroplanes which as fighters were already the fastest in the world were stripped of guns and fitted with cameras, nothing could possibly catch them so long as they operated from maximum altitude.

Cotton still remembers how Tedder listened with interest, but made few comments, and in due course suggested that the technicalities should be discussed with two of the Ministry's experts. Cotton was left with them, and they proceeded to explain at some length why it was impossible to equip the Spitfire with cameras. They insisted that the Blenheim was the only suitable aircraft.

Back in Tedder's office Cotton reported what had passed.

'If I were you,' said Tedder, 'I should take the Blenheim and prove that it will not do, and then have another shot.'

Cotton protested at the waste of time.

'I am very used to Service methods,' answered Tedder, 'and if you take my advice you will save a lot of time in the long run.'

So the Blenheim it was, and two were delivered to Heston a couple of days later: one on which to practise and the other for conversion.

Tedder had also given Cotton some helpful advice about arranging for modifications at the Royal Aircraft Establishment at Farnborough, and there he found a friend in Mr A.H. Hall, the Chief Superintendent. Hall was extremely interested when Cotton expounded his ideas about streamlining and polishing to increase speed, and agreed to give the Blenheims the full treatment at once.

In this way their speed was improved by about eighteen miles an hour, but this was still nothing approaching the performance that Cotton needed. Within a few weeks he was fighting for Spitfires again.

By this time Maurice Longbottom had joined the Heston Flight, and Cotton found in him a very enthusiastic collaborator. 'Shorty' Longbottom's slide-rule mind became absorbed with the possibilities of using really high-speed aircraft for photographic reconnaissance and he was soon deep in performance figures. Together Cotton, Niven, and he thrashed out the whole project, and Cotton asked him to set down the arguments for the revolutionary new concept. The memorandum which he produced is a document of great historic interest. His summing-up reads as follows:

> The best method appears to be the use of a single small machine relying on its speed, climb, and ceiling to avoid destruction. A machine such as a single-seater fighter could fly high enough to be well above Ack-Ack fire and could rely upon sheer speed and height to get away from the enemy fighters. It would have no use for armament or radio and these could be removed to provide room for extra fuel, in order to get the necessary range. It would be a very small machine painted so as to reduce its visibility against the sky.

Thus with an accuracy which in retrospect is startling, was foretold the secret of the success which lay head.

●　　●　　●

Although the Heston Flight's speeded-up Blenheims were still not in the least up to Cotton's needs, they were soon being talked about at Fighter Command, and news of them came to the ears of the Commander-in-Chief, Air Chief Marshal Sir Hugh Dowding. The fighter version of the Blenheim that was being used for long-range patrols could do with some additional speed. So Dowding came over to Heston in person, and arrangements were made to 'Cottonize' eight of the fighter Blenheims right away. The work was rapidly completed, and the Commander-in-Chief was delighted: the performance of the long-range fighters was improved beyond his hopes, and he asked Cotton to see him at his Headquarters at Stanmore. Over a cup of tea he told him how satisfied he was, and added, 'Let me know if there is anything I can do for you at any time.'

Cotton says his throat went dry as he answered: 'There is one thing, sir. Do you think you could lend me two Spitfires?'

'What do you want them for?'

With much earnestness Cotton explained his new concept of photographic reconnaissance. When he had finished, Dowding said: 'All right, I'll lend you two Spitfires, though you know they are beyond price to me. When would you like them?'

'Yesterday!' exclaimed Cotton.

Dowding smiled. 'Would nine o'clock tomorrow morning do?'

And sure enough, at nine o'clock the next morning two Spitfires landed at Heston.

The next thing was to get cameras installed, and Cotton set off immediately to see Hall at Farnborough. As at Harrogate, the experts who were first called in threw cold water on the whole project; but after they had gone, Hall said: 'We'll get on to Harry Stringer about this.'

Soon Cotton was closeted with Stringer, Farnborough's top expert on aerial cameras, and the two of them talked out the detail. Stringer was very enthusiastic. He was an old hand at the game; in fact he had been one of Moore-Brabazon's team of pioneers, and he was a natural technician of the highest order – 'he *always* knew where to drill the holes', as an admirer once put it. At the end of the First World War, when an automatic camera using film instead of plates first came into general use, Harry Stringer had helped to fit one into a single-seat aircraft – an omen for the future which between the wars was forgotten completely, except by Stringer himself and a very few others, Stringer had salvaged the remains of a crashed Spitfire, and had been experimenting with camera installations to see what could be done. Before Cotton arrived on the scene the idea had received little encouragement, but now he could really go ahead. He set to work with a will, and within a matter of days 'Shorty' Longbottom was flying a duck-egg green Spitfire back to Heston from Farnborough. Its guns had been removed, and there was a camera installed in each wing, in the manner which Cotton had found prevented them from freezing at high altitudes.

The moment was approaching for the first operational sortie, and Peck gave Cotton permission to make the necessary arrangements. So during the first week of November 1939 he was over in France conferring with the RAF chiefs in the British Expeditionary Force. He strongly believed that the headquarters of the Heston Flight should remain at Heston, largely on security grounds; and he planned to send to France a completely mobile unit which could be moved at a moment's notice to the operational base nearest to individual targets, thus overcoming some of the limitations of range. For the time being, until photographic trailers could be organized, the films would be flown back to England for processing.

The airfield at Seclin, near Lille, was chosen as a suitable starting-point, and without delay Spitfire N-3071 was brought over, accompanied by Longbottom and Niven. The detachment had to have some sort of title, so it was named the Special Survey Flight, but every possible precaution was taken to conceal its activities. At the airfield the Spitfire was kept in its own private hangar under lock and key; and Cotton insisted that the two pilots should not mix with the

RAF units in France, so Niven and Longbottom kept to themselves in a local hotel. The pilots of the squadrons at Seclin could catch a glimpse of the solitary pale green Spitfire as it landed and took off, but they could only wonder and guess what it was up to.

On 18 November the great moment came. At 1 p.m. Longbottom took off from Seclin, bound for the German border and Aachen. The sortie was unsuccessful in the sense that he did not reach his targets; but he *did* take several runs of good photographs from 33,000 feet over Europe and the country just west of the frontier itself. It was a historic occasion: for the first time successful exposures had been made at high altitude under war conditions by cameras mounted in a Spitfire. Hopes were fast turning into facts, and the dream of taking photographs unseen and unchallenged in wartime was now a reality. The new photographic intelligence had been launched on its meteoric course.

Two days later Longbottom photographed actual German ground, but then the weather closed in, and from the third week of November till mid December not a sortie could be made because of fog and snow. During the last days of 1939, however, and the first week of the new year, there were a few cloudless days and the two pilots made good use of them. Many sorties were flown from Lille and from the Essey airfield near Nancy; Cologne and Düsseldorf were photographed, and large areas of the Siegfried Line were 'covered' for the first time.

Cotton was constantly coming over from Heston, for there was much to discuss and arrange. The flights were always planned with meticulous care, but in certain ways the pilots had to discover what planning was needed as they went along, for they were working in circumstances without precedent. They soon found, for instance, that condensation trails – the long 'white plumes' as they called them – were going to be a very serious matter for 'invisible' photographic planes; and the effects of high altitude on the pilots themselves raised many new problems. Cotton hastened to ask for a medical officer to be attached to the Heston Flight, for, as he put it, 'What we are doing today the fighters will be doing tomorrow, the bombers the day after tomorrow, and civilian aircraft after the war.'

•   •   •

As Longbottom and Niven flew sortie after sortie, the difficulty of getting their photographs interpreted became very acute, and Cotton looked around for a new solution. Obviously Walter Heath and his few helpers at the Air Ministry could not be expected to cope with this influx, and Sidney turned to a friend of his who had worked with him in Newfoundland in the early twenties, Major 'Lemnos' Hemming, who was still in the aerial survey business and was managing director of a firm called the Aircraft Operating Company. Cotton knew that he had acquired for his company an elaborate Swiss machine for recording precise measurements from aerial photographs, and this might well provide an answer, or at least a partial one. Early in December 1939 Cotton explained the situation to him, and together they agreed to experiment. The whole thing would have to be completely unofficial, for although Hemming had been well aware what his firm might contribute to British intelligence, and had, in fact, already been in touch with the Air Ministry, nothing definite had come of it.

On 7 December 1939, Cotton handed over to Hemming a set of five-inch-square photographs, without vouchsafing any information as to where, when, or how they had been taken, and just said: 'See how much information you can get out of them.' Hemming took them at once to his brilliant photogrammetric expert, Michael Spender, brother of Stephen Spender the poet and Humphrey Spender the artist, who was soon hard at work on them. Spender was thus brought into touch with photographic intelligence, as distinct from pure aerial survey. Before long he was to become one of the greatest influences on the development of interpretation in the early part of the war. Aerial photographs had first deeply interested him when, after leaving Oxford, he took part in several expeditions as a geographer – first in Greenland, and then on a preliminary Everest survey. Later he learnt how to operate the photogrammetric machines of the Swiss company named Wild (pronounced 'Vilt') and shortly before the war he had joined Hemming's staff.

On the day after the photographs had been handed over, early in the afternoon, a powerful-looking red car drew up outside the little factory at Wembley where the drawing-offices and dark rooms of the Aircraft Operating Company were installed. Kelson, the chauffeur, jumped out and opened the door for Sidney Cotton – tall, quick, wolf-like, with horn-rimmed glasses and thick grey-white hair. In the managing director's office he was greeted by a thickset man with a slightly piratical look; 'Lemnos' Hemming had blinded one eye in an aeroplane crash and always wore a black eye-patch. Cotton produced a roll of film. 'I've brought some more,' he said. 'How are you getting on?' 'Come and see,' said Hemming.

The small room where Spender was working was dominated by the huge Wild machine. Its massive grey-green frame, shaped like an arch and higher than a man, supported the intricacies of the main mechanism; and Michael Spender, in his shirt-sleeves, was sitting on a high stool in front of it, gazing intently at some transparencies through an apparatus that looked something like binoculars. Though the viewing mechanism, which worked on the same principle as a simple stereoscope, he could see everything in three dimensions; and with the machine's infinitely fine pointer, he was touching – carefully, deliberately – the points in the image which he needed to record in order to make his measurements. Meanwhile, on a paper-covered table alongside, a pencil on a long arm, connected with the pointer, was recording the relative position of every point precisely to scale.

'How's it going?' asked Hemming.

Spender looked up. 'The scale's absurdly small,' he said, 'which isn't surprising as I find the photographs were taken from 34,000 feet. It's a fantastic height. But I'm getting quite a lot out of them. I can plot and measure anything as long as I can see its outline.'

'That Wild gives nine times magnification,' put in Hemming.

'Don't worry about scale just now,' said Cotton. 'We've got to use the tools that are available. The cameras that took those photographs were meant to be operated at 8,000 feet. But it won't be long before we have something better. New lenses and new cameras too.' He looked at the pencilled marks on the paper-covered table. 'I see you can measure some of the buildings all right,' he said, and then after a moment's pause he added, 'and there's no reason why you shouldn't measure ships.'

'No,' replied Spender, 'if I could see their outlines I could measure them.'

Ships! That was what Cotton had been hoping for most of all. Something for the Naval Intelligence Division. As soon as he could put long-range tanks into one of the Spitfires, the ships of the German fleet at their home bases could be counted, measures, identified.

TWO

TRIAL AND ERROR

'No prophet is accepted in his own country.' This truth held good, in an inter-Service context, even when the prophet was a consummate schemer and an inexhaustible worker like Sidney Cotton. It held good even when, early in 1940, his prophecies were being transmuted into hard facts. From certain Air Force officers Cotton received heartfelt sympathy as be battled ahead for equipment and facilities and personnel; but on the whole it was from outside 'the family' that help and encouragement came: from the Admiralty, from the Army in France, and from the French themselves.

Very early on Cotton had discovered that the assurance of a 'free hand', the condition on which he had agreed to work within the RAF, was not a magic formula that could eliminate the creaking and grinding of a big administrative machine being forced into wartime expansion; nevertheless he was so utterly convinced of the importance of his work that he rebelled against the slightest delay. He always thought of every detail, and his demands were unceasing, but equipment of every kind was, of course, in very short supply. 'It's worse than trying to extract diamonds from the Crown Jewels,' Cotton wrote to an influential friend whose help he was trying to enlist.

Results did come, however, little by little. Never as quickly as Cotton would have liked, and not always in the way he wanted, but they came. For instance, in the matter of the pressing need for redesigned cameras and lenses. In January 1940 Wing Commander Victor Laws, then chief photographic officer with the British Expeditionary Force, was brought back from France to form a new Air Ministry department, especially to steer photographic research and development, and to organize supplies. Laws had been working with aerial cameras for nearly thirty years, for in 1912 he had taken photographs from airships and man-carrying kites, and during the First World War he was one of Moore-Brabazon's foremost helpers. From 1940 onwards, throughout the war, he was in a position to take a lead in pushing for better photographic quality and for an adequate supply of equipment.

Cotton was always in and out of the Air Ministry for visits and meetings, and he followed them up with a non-stop barrage of letters (he had three Dictaphones: one in the Lockheed, one in his car, and one at Heston). A Group Captain and a Wing Commander were appointed to deal with this typewritten offensive, and to act as a buffer between Cotton and the Air Staff. There was no ill feeling, but quite a lot of plain speaking, and one of their replies, bearing the date 5 February 1940, is worthy of record.

Nobody has yet questioned the excellent work which your unit has carried out with its very limited equipment. One reason, however, why the establishment which you submitted early in December was *not* immediately approved was that it contained certain items which Air Vice-Marshal Peck did not consider to be warranted by the work you were undertaking. As a business man you are just as well aware as I am that no Corporation is in a position to give a 'blank cheque' on all occasions!

Finally, I would remind you that we are all of us part of a machine, which has gathered considerable momentum (although it may not have appeared to you to have done so) since the outbreak of war; and every member of it, without exception, is fully aware how valuable time is when faced with an enemy who is quite prepared to take advantage of our delays.

This last may sound like a platitude, but I can assure you that considering the somewhat unusual manner in which Number 2 Camouflage Unit* was brought into being, the priority which it has received compares *most favourably* with any other unit which I know in the RAF. Even today, as you know, you are receiving quite exceptional treatment in regard to the supply both of personnel and also of material.

At the end of the letter there was a postscript as follows: 'You need not bother to send your answer to this – I know it. It is "God save the rest of the Air Force".' Needless to say, however, Cotton did send an answer – pages of it, by return – stressing once more in no uncertain terms that the impossible *must* be achieved; that during the months of procrastination more and more Blenheims and their crews were being lost. He wound up with the comment:

Yes, the unfortunate birth of the Unit may have had a lot to do with the delays, but now that we have a kicking child, let us feed it properly.

One of Cotton's most trusted and helpful friends in the RAF was Air Marshal Sir Arthur Barratt, with whom he had been in touch since the early days of the Heston Flight, and at the beginning of 1940, 'Ugly' Barratt's position as commander of the British Air Forces in France made him a powerful ally. It was to Barratt that Cotton

* In November 1939 the Heston Flight's name was changed to 'No. 2 Camouflage Unit', for security reasons; and in mid-January 1940 the name was again changed to 'The Photographic Development Unit', though the old name was still sometimes used.

turned for advice about one of his most urgent problems: he desperately needed a really good second-in-command, a regular Air Force officer who could be relied upon to run things wisely and efficiently while he was over in France, and would know how to cope with all the Service routine. With Barratt's help the perfect man for the job was found, but it was a fight to get him. Cotton persevered, however, and eventually succeeded in arranging for Squadron Leader Geoffrey Tuttle, DFC, to be posted to Heston.

Barratt and Cotton had many long talks about the best way to operate the new photographic reconnaissance and from these discussions emerged a plan for expanding the system of mobile units in France. Each Flight would have a Spitfire, a Hudson to carry spares and servicing crew, and several vehicles, including a mobile wireless unit. It thus would be completely mobile and self-contained. This plan was put to the Air Staff and accepted; and later, when the set-up began to take actual shape, it was given official status as No. 212 Squadron. It was also agreed that Cotton should have an advanced headquarters near Barratt, who was at Coulommiers, thirty-seven miles east of Paris.

At Tigeaux, a quiet little village twelve minutes from Barratt's headquarters, Cotton found just what he wanted: the Old Mill, a good-sized but inconspicuous villa. He rented it privately so as to be 'independent', and protected it from the curious by putting up notice boards to announce that it had been taken over as a rest-home for convalescents. Tigeaux was his choice not only because it was near Coulommiers; it was also only a few miles from Meaux, the headquarters of the French Chief of Air Staff.

During the early weeks of 1940, Sidney's splendid Hotch-kiss saloon, RAF X, with a small Union Jack on its number-plate which lit up at night, was often over at Meaux; and soon he had a *carte blanche* letter from General Vuillemin, assuring him of all possible cooperation from the French Air Force.

At Meaux was also the main centre of French photographic interpretation, and Cotton immediately got into touch with Colonel Lespair, the officer-in-charge. On his first visit, in January 1940, he was at once very much impressed. Lespair showed him the beautiful dossiers full of photographs of the Siegfried Line, annotated in white ink, and as Cotton glanced through some of the interpretations, and noticed the detail of the analyses, he realized that there was much to learn from the French. When Lespair offered to give him any help he might need, he jumped at the chance, and within a few days a young Pilot Officer named Douglas Kendall had been sent out from Heston and was taking the French interpretation course. Like many of Cotton's moves, this arrangement meant more for the future than was obvious at the time. Douglas Kendall, who before the war had been in aerial survey, working for a branch of the Aircraft Operating Company in Africa, later became one of the foremost interpreters of photographs in the whole war, and that early training at Meaux may have had something to do with it. But Kendall's natural ability for deductive reasoning and analysis, along with his calm persistence and capacity for unending work, were the things that really counted. Cotton had backed yet another winner.

It soon proved that the French were also going to profit from the liaison at Meaux, for some of the early Spitfire photographs showed parts of the Siegfried Line they themselves had never succeeded in covering. At first the French interpreters were somewhat dismayed by the small scale, but they quickly realized that this 'basic cover' was invaluable to them. Small scale is, in point of fact, a definite advantage in the very first cover of any area, for it means that the whole lie of the land can be reviewed – provided that later sorties can be flown to get larger scale photographs for investigating detail and activity.

Lespair was genuinely keen to help Cotton along, and he had a very impressive chart made in order to help him present his case in London. It showed the following statistics for the period since war began till the middle of January 1940:

The RAF had photographed 2,500 square miles of enemy territory with a loss of 40 aircraft.

The French had photographed 6,000 square miles with a loss of 60 aircraft.

The detachment from Heston had photographed 5,000 square miles without losing the one and only Spitfire that had done the whole job.

On 26 January 1940, when Cotton produced this chart at the Air Ministry, he expatiated on the theme: 'The Messerschmitts haven't a chance against the Spitfire because of its speed and altitude. And all that can be seen from the ground is an occasional condensation trail very high up.' He had been arguing on these lines for weeks, but the French chart certainly put it in a nutshell, and perhaps it helped to tip the scale; for a few days later the Air Council at last accepted the proposals to expand the Photographic Development Unit.

●　　●　　●

Although much of Cotton's time was spent nipping over to France in the Lockheed, flying in any sort of weather, dressed sometimes as a Wing Commander and sometimes as a civilian, there was also much of the utmost importance to be done in London, not only at the Air Ministry. In the Naval Intelligence Division, Sidney Cotton was always a welcome visitor. He did not, of course, have to battle with the Admiralty about equipment and policy, and he found the naval intelligence officers ardently encouraging, and only too willing to help him in any way they could.

The Admiralty had to depend entirely on the RAF for photographic reconnaissance, for although control of the Fleet Air Arm had been transferred to them in 1937, it had been laid down that the Navy should not operate land-based aircraft. So the tragic failure of the Blenheims was an extremely serious matter to the Naval Staff, and Cotton became their blue-eyed boy who could be relied on to deliver the goods.

In February 1940 the whole thing came to a head. The Admiralty was clamouring for cover of Wilhelmshaven, as they were very anxious to know whether the *Tirpitz* was really out of graving dock, as reported by other intelligence sources. But the Blenheims had failed to provide the answer. By this time the Photographic Development Unit had a total of four Spitfires, and one of them had been fitted with an additional tank, giving range enough to reach Wilhelmshaven.

10 February was a cold, clear day, and just before eleven o'clock 'Shorty' Longbottom climbed into the cockpit of the new Spitfire. In the converted fighter, which was stripped of all non-essentials, and polished to a nicety, he could climb to nearly twice as high as the Blenheims, and his top speed was more than 100 miles an hour better than theirs. Soon after three o'clock he was back at Heston, safe but frozen stiff, having photographed both Emden and Wilhelmshaven from more than five miles up.

The eagerly awaited moment had now come to try out the Wild machine for measuring ships on the Spitfire photographs. By this time there was a regular arrangement that all the Heston sorties should be sent to Wembley for interpretation, but the work was still a 'private venture'. As soon as the transparencies were ready, Michael Spender was busy on them, and almost at once he could report that the *Tirpitz* was still in graving dock after all. He could also discern important details concerning the layout of the battleships.

Spender had always been fascinated by ships. Even as a

boy he used to think of them in terms of structure related to form, and it came naturally to him to pursue this interest when his work for Hemming began to involve him in intelligence. But the value of Michael Spender's early research in shipping interpretation would not have been as great as it was unless it had been shared – right from the beginning – with an officer of the Admiralty's Naval Intelligence Division, Lieutenant-Commander 'Ned' Denning, who could bring to the work the approach of the trained intelligence officer, as well as a specialized knowledge of enemy ships. He was often at Wembley and he and Spender together began to discover, little by little, what a vast amount of information about ships can be derived from aerial photographs.

The detailed interpretation of the ships themselves was not, however, the main undertaking on the photographs that Longbottom brought back on 10 February. The sort of work for which 'the Wild' was primarily designed was the making of maps and plans, and within forty-eight hours Spender had produced superb plans of the port of Emden, and of the naval base at Wilhelmshaven, with all the ships delineated to scale.

When Admiral Godfrey received these plans he decided to show them at once to the Chief of Naval Staff, and presently they were being shown to the First Lord himself. Mr Churchill was very much interested and was surprised to learn that it had been necessary to do the work 'unofficially'. His comments started off a rapid chain of events.

Cotton was immediately summoned to the Admiralty and told that the Chief of Naval Staff wanted to see him personally. Sir Dudley Pound explained that certain plans for an urgent operation depended entirely on knowing where various units of the German Navy were stationed. He pointed out the places where the ships might be, and asked Cotton if it was possible to photograph them.

'Yes, sir,' replied Cotton. 'The Spitfire with extra range could easily cover all those points in one flight.'

Pound was delighted, and said he wanted Cotton to attend the War Room meeting that evening, as he planned to take up the whole question with the Air Staff.

'Do you really think it wise for me to be present?' asked Cotton. 'If the Air Staff resent my being there, they could post me and take over my unit, and then you'd be as badly off as before I started. It would be a pity to antagonize them when things seem to be moving at last. The Air Council has just agreed that I should have eight more Spitfires.'

'I'll discuss it with the First Lord,' said Pound. 'It was he who asked me to see you.'

Later Cotton was told that he was definitely wanted at the meeting and at nine-thirty sharp he arrived at the Admiralty War Room, where he was welcomed by Pound. A few minutes later, however, Air Vice-Marshal Peirse entered the room. He was naturally amazed to see Cotton there, and asked him what he was doing. Pound intervened, and explained that they had sent for Cotton in a hurry, and there had been no time to ask the Air Staff if he might attend. 'We hope he may be able to help on a matter we're going to discuss this evening.' Pound, as Chief of Naval Staff, took the high-backed chair at the head of the table, and he signalled to Cotton to sit on his right hand, in the place which was normally reserved for the senior RAF officer present. Cotton obediently took the place of honour, but he remembers vividly that he hardly dared to look in Peirse's direction.

For two hours the sore question of the Admiralty's need for photographs of the German Fleet was discussed from every angle. Cotton had brought copies of the new Wild plans with him, and they were duly produced and handed round. Everyone agreed they were magnificent, and Peirse himself asked how such good results were obtained.

'With a special photogrammetric machine,' replied Cotton.

'Why wasn't I told about it?' asked Peirse. 'I would have requisitioned it at once.'

At last, when it was nearly midnight, Pound said he was not prepared to accept any further delays, and looking straight at Peirse he said: 'So may we ask Cotton's unit to get the information we need?' When Peirse had agreed, Pound turned to Cotton.

'You have heard what we've been discussing. Can you get the information?'

'Yes, sir,' replied Cotton, 'quite easily.'

At nine o'clock the next morning, Cotton was with Peirse at the Air Ministry.

'I want to know all about the photogrammetric equipment you mentioned last night,' said Peirse. 'What is it, and where is it?'

'The equipment belongs to the Aircraft Operating Company,' replied Cotton. 'It is the equipment which Hemming has been trying to persuade the Air Ministry to take over ever since the beginning of the war. I've had to make use of it privately so as to give the Admiralty the interpretations they need.'

Peirse agreed then and there to requisition the Wild machine, and also agreed that the Aircraft Operating Company should be formally amalgamated with the Air Ministry's interpretation section.

The Admiralty was taking no chances, however. Shortly after the War Room meeting Mr Churchill wrote to the Secretary of State for Air, Sir Kingsley Wood, on the subject of the excellent photogrammetric work which had just been shown to him. He made his views on the subject very clear:

Major Hemming's organization, including the expert personnel, should be taken over by one of the Service departments without delay . . . If for any reason the Air Ministry do not wish to take it over, we should be quite prepared to do so.

After this the wheels began to turn slowly, and six weeks later Hemming finally received a letter to say that the Air Ministry would like to negotiate a contract.

•　　•　　•

In the early months of 1940 the factory at Wembley and the Air Ministry's small section under Walter Heath were not the only places in England where the art of photographic interpretation was being practised. At Bomber Command's new underground headquarters near High Wycombe there was a photographic intelligence section – well organized and neat, with a fine little array of map racks, interpreters' desks, and frames for viewing transparencies. Air Chief Marshal Sir Edgar Ludlow-Hewitt, then Commander-in-Chief, had decided in 1938 to develop this branch of intelligence at his headquarters. He knew at first hand what aerial photography had achieved in the First World War, and more recently he had been impressed by its potentialities when he was commanding the RAF in India between 1935 and 1937. There his interest had been shared by his personal assistant, Flight Lieutenant Peter Riddell, and when he started up the new Bomber Command section he arranged for Riddell to come and organize it.

The plan was that the photographs obtained by Bomber Command's reconnaissance Blenheims should be sent on to the headquarters after the Station Intelligence Officers had taken a quick look at them; and the function of the headquarters section was to supply certain target material and to report on bomb damage in detail. But the trouble was, of course, that the Blenheims could not obtain more than a few of the covers that were needed. Some of the early photographs of targets in north-west Germany bear witness to the fearlessness and perseverance of the Blenheim pilots; but Bomber Command, like the Admiralty, was constantly being frustrated by lack of photographs, while crew after crew was lost and the cameras froze up with fiendish regularity. Cotton knew all about this; and he also knew the paramount importance Bomber Command attached to the plan for the bombing of the Ruhr.

Towards the end of February 1940 a Spitfire with yet another additional tank was ready, but day after day of solid cloud kept it on the ground. Then at last on 2 March the weather was right, and Bob Niven took off from Heston bound for the Ruhr. At 30,000 feet above Duisburg he started his cameras and flew eastward above the Ruhr valley as far as Dortmund. He looked back, and down, and all round: not an Me 109 anywhere. He banked right over, and turned for a run back to the Rhine, flying parallel to his previous run so as to cover the whole of the industrial area. He kept his cameras on right up to the German frontier; then turned south for the trek round the edge of Holland and Belgium and so home. Over the hills and woods of Luxembourg the German fighters put in an appearance at last, three of them. Niven opened right up and felt as if he had been given a blow in the back as the Spitfire leapt forward. When he looked back the Messerschmitts were out of sight.

Niven's photographs were exactly what Cotton had hoped for, and he had already made his plans how to use them. This was an occasion when not only a detailed plan but a 'mosaic' could best serve his purpose, because when the overlapping prints were pieced together by the interpreters and rephotographed, the full extent of the cover could be displayed with dramatic effect. When Sidney unrolled his great mosaic of the Ruhr before Ludlow-Hewitt, and stood back triumphantly, the Commander-in-Chief's long face seemed to grow longer than ever, and by silence he showed his amazed delight. Cotton then hastened to explain what difficulties he was having about equipment, and Ludlow-Hewitt gladly assured him that he would do all he could to help. In actual fact he went much further, for he immediately made a proposal to the Air Ministry that Bomber Command should take over the Photographic Development Unit. But the proposal was turned down.

The main issue was one of priorities. Whose needs for photographic intelligence should come first? Every day the Admiralty and the Air Staff in France were competing for Cotton's services, and if Bomber Command were in charge everyone else would have to take a back seat. Better for the Air Ministry to keep the reins. So the existing pattern continued for the time being, though the pattern itself was one of constant change. At Bomber Command, however, the idea of its own independent photographic reconnaissance unit was not abandoned, and eight months later the Command did for a time possess its own high-flying photographic Spitfires – but that is a story that comes later.

Four days after Niven's Ruhr sortie, he and Longbottom were awarded DFCs, and there was much rejoicing within the Photographic Development Unit. But Cotton was horrified when he found that *The Aeroplane* and *Flight*, in announcing the awards, had quoted the following official statement:

> Both of the officers have been pioneers in a new method of aerial photography, and have taken overlapping photographs of many enemy defences.

A letter protesting about this 'most undesirable publicity' went off at once to Peck; but within the unit Cotton had no cause to complain of any lack of indiscretion. At about this time he conferred upon certain of his team a secret badge, bearing the cryptic symbols. 'CC11'. Only the initiated knew that 'CC' stood for 'Cotton's Crooks', a nickname which originated because some of the Heston personnel were very good at acquiring things without going through official channels, while '11' referred to the 'eleventh' commandment: 'Thou shalt not be found out.'

The hand-picked team at Heston had been growing gradually. Geoffrey Tuttle was at first the only RAF regular officer, but a number of very useful men had been roped in from civil life. An early arrival was Hugh Macphail, an adventurous pilot of the First World War, who in 1939 had been flying for a Peruvian airline. He had hurried back to England and was soon a Squadron Leader at Heston, acting as Cotton's personal assistant. Paul Lamboit, who arrived safely from America in response to Cotton's cable, appeared somewhat shyly at Heston in the uniform of a Pilot Officer. When Cotton saw him he said: 'I can't possibly have a Pilot Officer in charge of my photo section. You'd better get some more braid and put up Squadron Leader's rings.' Lamboit did as he was told, and the necessary formalities were completed at the Air Ministry 'in due course'.

Most of Cotton's new pilots were young officers from various RAF squadrons in France, who had come forward in response to an appeal for volunteers with navigational experience to fly 'something very fast', and several of these, such as Alistair Taylor, Spencer Ring, and 'Bill' Wise, were soon to become outstanding in photographic reconnaissance. Rather in a class by himself, however, was Flying Officer Slocum, a carefree young man who had formerly been an airline pilot. He joined the Air Force at the beginning of the war, and was stationed at a Scottish base; but he enjoyed flying for Cotton, and without asking anyone's permission he used to slip down to Heston, do a photographic flight or two, and then return to his squadron. Eventually his commanding officer got tired of this, and Slocum was officially posted to the Photographic Development Unit.

By early 1940, Cotton had several Hudsons fitted with cameras as well as the Spitfires, and in cloudy weather Slocum used to go off in one of these, briefed to break cloud precisely at the right moment to photograph his target, and in this way he got some very valuable results. Early in March, however, he met a tragic end, for his Hudson was mistaken for a German plane by British fighters and was shot down over Kent.

•   •   •

Cotton was not content with convincing the Air Force, the Admiralty, and the French of the necessity for the new photographic intelligence. It was obvious to him that the Army needed it just as badly. At this stage the British Army's photographic reconnaissance was in a plight somewhat similar to the Air Force's. The army cooperation squadrons, equipped with Blenheims and Lysanders, were suffering terrible losses, and the photographs which did come back were normally interpreted by intelligence officers. In the Army, as in the RAF, the need for specialists had not been foreseen, and in the whole of the BEF there were, at first, only two photographic interpreters: Major Tom Churchill and Lieutenant Gerald Lacoste, who were both attached to Lord Gort's headquarters at Arras. Their main work was preparing annotated maps of the Siegfried Line defences.

Into this Army stronghold one day early in 1940 came Air Marshal Barratt, accompanied by Sidney Cotton with an enormous album under his arm. In Lord Gort's office Cotton turned the pages and showed off enlargements from his five best sorties, complete with beautifully annotated transparent overlays. He pointed to a stretch of river on one of the photographs. 'The defences are very heavy on this bit of the Rhine, as you see,' he said, 'but the Spitfire was far above anti-aircraft range.'

The idea of Cotton's special brand of photographic reconnaissance was a new one to the Army, but the Army's response to it was not slow. Already the threat of a German invasion of Belgium was a very real one, and the maps of Belgium were hopelessly out of date. This new high-altitude photography, in spite of its small scale, would be invaluable for correcting them, and who was to say whether a Spitfire at 30,000 feet was technically infringing neutrality? Gort and Barratt were equally enthusiastic, and Cotton was given orders to go ahead. In mid March 1940 when a Flight of 212 Squadron began operating from Lille, its official targets were supposed to be in Germany, but on a great many of the flights the pilots were 'dogged by compass trouble', and as a result of these 'misfortunes' it was not long before the whole of Belgium had been photographed.

Eventually, when the Air Staff got to hear about the 'X' series of sorties, as the cover of Belgium was called, Cotton was severely criticized for photographing neutral territory. But with undaunted spirits he later maintained: 'What we were mixed up in was a war we had to win – not a parlour game.' Thus, in a typically unorthodox manner, he helped to set the pattern for the future. For one of the lessons of the Second World War was to be that photographic intelligence must be able to serve more than one master – more than one Command – more than one Service – indeed more than one Ally.

•   •   •

While the flying went ahead from Lille, and soon also from the airfield at Essey near Nancy, a longer-range Spitfire was being prepared at Farnborough, and by 7 April 1940 it was ready. At the Admiralty's special request, Kiel was its first objective. But even with the extra tank there was not enough fuel to get to Kiel and back from Heston, so Longbottom refuelled at a Norfolk airfield, and then took off for the Baltic. Four hours later Cotton and Tuttle sighed with relief as they heard the Spitfire overhead, and 'Shorty' came taxying in, numb and frozen, and with hardly a drop of fuel left. There had been some trouble with cameras, but he had succeeded in photographing Kiel.

At Wembley that night, Spender and Denning measured and analysed and discussed. Kiel harbour was crammed to overflowing with shipping. At the nearby Holtenau airfield, too, there were swarms of Ju 52s. But as Kiel had never been photographed before, who could say that this was not its normal state? The whole thing was actually, of course, exceptionally abnormal, for 7 April was two days before the invasion of Denmark and Norway. But Spender and Denning could do no more than report the invasion fleets as though they were an everyday sight. That is what it means to have to interpret activity from a single photographic cover.

During the months that followed that first cover of Kiel, Michael Spender made perhaps his greatest contribution to the technique of photographic interpretation by reaffirming the basic principle of comparing consecutive covers. During the First World War it had come to be accepted as axiomatic that the value of evidence from a sequence of covers far transcends the evidence of a single sortie; but in the new circumstances of the Second World War it needed someone of Spender's calibre to put across the idea that aerial photography can yield information in time as well as in space.

The new developments of photographic intelligence, and everyone concerned with them, were to be put severely to the test before the spring of 1940 was out. On the morning of 10 May, while the Germans swept forward into the Low Countries, Sidney Cotton hurried from office to office at the Air Ministry. Later he wrote in his diary:

I think we see eye to eye now. As the war has really started, they will want our material more than ever, so we *must* have all the equipment we have requested and more.

That evening he flew over to France. The airfields at Lille and Nancy were already being bombed, so both Flights of 212 Squadron had evacuated to Meaux and Coulommiers according to plan, and arrangements for processing the films in photographic trailers were brought rapidly into effect. And to speed things up further, Kendall came to Tigeaux from the French unit at Meaux, so as to make immediate interpretations on the spot. The tempo of the war had accelerated so much that information more than a few hours old would be useless.

Barratt's photographic Blenheims, and also the obsolescent reconnaissance aircraft of the French Air Force, were doing their best in spite of shocking losses, but in the words of one of France's most illustrious authors, who was also a reconnaissance pilot at the time: 'It was as if you dashed glassfuls of water into a forest fire in the hope of putting it out.' Antoine de Saint-Exupéry was himself flying photographic sorties over the areas that the Germans had seized, and later, in *Flight to Arras*, he wrote:

> Fifty reconnaissance crews were all we had for the whole French army. Fifty crews of three men each, pilot, observer, and gunner. Out of the fifty, twenty-three made up our unit – Group 2–33. In three weeks, seventeen of the twenty-three had vanished. Our Group had melted like a lump of wax. . . . Fifty crews for the whole of France. The whole strategy of the French army rested upon our shoulders. An immense forest fire raging, and a hope that it might be put out by the sacrifice of a few glassfuls of water.

No wonder that as soon as the German onrush began, Barratt turned urgently to Cotton. During the 'phoney war' the latter's methods had succeeded where the orthodox reconnaissance had failed. Perhaps even now he could work a miracle with his few Spitfires.

Anything that could be done *had* to be done – and at once. Every possible scrap of information on the enemy advance was needed.

Early on 15 May 1940, Barratt's intelligence staff were in dire need of information about the Dinant area, and at eleven o'clock Flight Lieutenant Pippet, who acted as liaison officer between Tigeaux and the headquarters, waited anxiously at the Meaux airfield for the return of one of the Spitfires. Almost as soon as the films were out of the aeroplane he was tearing back to Tigeaux with them. The two photographic trailers were parked alongside a chateau not far from the Old Mill, and a sergeant named Walton, who was in charge, was waiting outside with Kendall. They all hurried inside into the blackness, and Walton's men got to work on processing the films. Above the door a single red light gave a faint glow.

'They just don't know what they're asking,' said Kendall to Pippet, 'if they *must* have the answers in a matter of seconds there's no time for prints. I'll have to do my best with the wet negatives. So I can't use a stereoscope. It's mad, absolutely mad, but there's no time for anything else. I've talked with Walton, and he's going to turn the film slowly on the drum and stop when I tell him; then I'll interpret what I can, and you jot it down and go and phone headquarters. Okay?'

While the German armour began its main westward advance from the Sedan bridgehead, Kendall's magnifier was focused on the breakthrough forty miles to the north, as he struggled to discern the detail on the photographs, which had been taken from about 30,000 feet. 'Bridge at Dinant not destroyed,' Pippet scribbled. 'Mechanized traffic crossing. Considerable numbers of mechanized vehicles moving up to bridge along Dinant-Spontin road throughout its length, i.e. 3 kilometres.'

'I'd better phone this right away,' he said. 'You go ahead with the next lot and I'll be back.'

An hour later Pippet was at the telephone for the

second time. 'Bridge at Anhée not destroyed. Mechanized traffic moving up Purnod–Yvoir road. Railway bridges across main roads in this district destroyed. Large bodies of mechanized traffic have moved across country leaving tracks . . .'

A little later he was on the phone to Barratt's headquarters for a third time, reading out Kendall's final interpretation to Pilot Officer Ian Parsons: 'Heavy bombing north-east of Mezières. Aerodrome hit by numerous bombs, but still usable.'

Five years later, when Wing Commander Kendall used to give his regular lecture on photographic intelligence at the RAF Staff College, he always laid emphasis on the dangers as well as the great advantages of this form of intelligence. 'Photographic evidence is positive and undeniable,' he would point out in his quiet convincing way, 'and it therefore enables positive counter action to be taken – in fact demands it; but this is dangerous when you can only see part of the whole picture, because it almost inevitably causes the wrong emphasis in counter measures. If a directing headquarters sees a photograph of a bridge that needs blowing up, the natural tendency is to lay on operations to attack it, without in fact knowing whether it is the right target in relation to the over-all battle, simply because sufficient over-all information is not available. The answer, of course, is to have enough reconnaissance aircraft and interpreters, and a properly geared organization to provide a total picture.'

But on the evening of 15 May 1940, as Pilot Officer Kendall, white and exhausted, steadied his nerves with a double brandy, all he could say to Pippet was: 'It's mad – absolutely mad!'

The next day an order came through from London that 212 Squadron was to be evacuated. Cotton immediately appealed to Barratt, and it was agreed that part of the unit should return to Heston, but that a nucleus should remain.

Since the Flights were mobile they could be moved home at the very last minute without causing trouble.

By this time the airfields east of Paris were being heavily bombed, and at midday on 17 May, as Cotton was on his way to Meaux to find out how things were going with Lespair and the French interpreters, he passed close to the Meaux airfield, which was in process of being bombed and also strafed by fighters. So he told his chauffeur, Kelson, to drive in under the trees near a deep ditch. The two of them stood beside the car for a little while, and then Cotton said: 'If the planes head in our direction you must jump into the ditch as quick as you can.'

'Will *you* get into the ditch also, sir?'

'Yes, Kelson, I certainly will.'

The perfect chauffeur hesitated for only a second and then asked: 'Shall I place the rug in the ditch, sir?'

When Barratt's headquarters withdrew to Orleans, a Flight of 212 Squadron moved with him, and for a final few days it operated from a nearby airfield. But Cotton's Spitfires were already hard at work taking photographs from French bases much further afield. As soon as the German invasion began, Cotton had asked Barratt for permission to arrange with the French to operate from bases on the Riviera. For it seemed certain that Italy would come into the war at any moment, and it was therefore very important to photograph the Brenner Pass and various other important objectives. So throughout the second half of May 1940 and the first half of June, Longbottom and several other pilots flew sorties from Le Luc and Hyères, and also from a Corsican airfield. And while Cotton was constantly back and forth between the south of France and Barratt's headquarters, Geoffrey Tuttle kept things going at Heston, organizing the flying programme in an attempt to meet the pressing demands of the Air Staff, the Admiralty, and Bomber Command. All three needed frequent covers of targets in France, Belgium, and Holland – all on the highest priority – and equipment was pitifully short.

Meantime a dreadful crisis faced Lord Gort's photographic intelligence officers at Arras, for when the moment came to evacuate, their whole print library had to be destroyed at a few hours' notice. Gerald Lacoste tried frantically to make a bonfire of the stacks of shiny prints, but they all stuck together and would not burn. He threw paraffin over them, but it only flared up and blackened the edges of the photographs and then went out. He was poking desperately when another interpretation officer, Captain Walter Venour, came hurrying up: 'We've got to move – this minute!'

'But we can't,' said Lacoste, poking some more.

'We'll just have to bring it with us,' replied Venour, and between them they shovelled the smouldering mountain into the back of an old army car. At their next stop the photographs were shovelled out and Lacoste tried to light his bonfire again; but only after two more moves had he got rid of the last of it.

Cotton managed to keep up the photographic sorties from French bases till the very end; but after the Germans entered Paris, on 14 June 1940, the final move back to England obviously could not be postponed much longer. It was from an airfield near La Rochelle that the last of 212 Squadron left for England, via the Channel Islands, on 16 June. Kendall and Pippet and Walton were there, and Belcher the equipment officer and also Kelson. Sidney Cotton himself was one of the last to leave. But as he flew the Lockheed G-AFTL back across the English Channel for the last time, accompanied by an English girl and her dog – they had been left stranded in Nantes – he little knew what he was going to find awaiting him at Heston.

THREE

THE INVASION THREAT

Britain had faced the threat of invasion before – time after time during the past thousand years – but never before 1940 had British eyes been able to watch the assembly of an entire invasion fleet. Photographic intelligence was the new factor that made this possible. At the time when the enemy was preparing for the cross-Channel assault, most of the normal methods of obtaining information were unworkable; and the photographs were recognized, both by the Chiefs of Staff and by everyone else concerned, as the one and only reliable source.

Thus the summer of 1940 was the first great proving time for the new photographic intelligence. It was also a time of rapid expansion and change both at Heston and Wembley; for the fall of France brought home to everyone concerned the desperate necessity for reconnaissance. On 10 June, just a week after Dunkirk, while Sidney Cotton was still working on untiringly in France, the whole question of the status of the Photographic Development Unit was raised at a high-level inter-Service meeting in London. The meeting went on for hours: it seemed impossible to find a way of sharing out the fruits of the unit's tiny resources among its hungry customers.

With the likelihood of German invasion looming ahead, the Admiralty demanded that all its efforts should be devoted to watching enemy ports; but Bomber Command would not accept this, as they considered the bombing programme an integral part of anti-invasion measures and had urgent need of sorties for damage assessment. The suggestion that Bomber Command should control the photographic unit was raised afresh but not accepted: if the unit went to Bomber Command, the Admiralty might be driven to setting up its own organization. Within a few days the Air Staff found a solution. Coastal Command was already in charge of the Air Force's visual reconnaissance of enemy shipping; its ties with the Admiralty were close and the Commander-in-Chief, Air Chief Marshal Sir Frederick Bowhill, was much interested in nautical matters. What could be more appropriate than to give the photographic unit to Coastal, when its prime responsibility was to be a watch on the invasion ports? Besides, the whole scope of its work was to be expanded; forward bases were to be started up in northern Scotland and in Cornwall, so as to bring a vast stretch of enemy coastline within range. The moment had evidently come to establish the unit on a regular Air Force footing.

So when Sidney Cotton arrived back at Heston on 17 June, he was handed a letter from the Air Ministry. It was signed by Sir Arthur Street, the Permanent Under-Secretary of State for Air, and read as follows:

Sir,

I am commanded by the Air Council to inform you that they have recently had under review the question of the future status and organization of the Photographic Development Unit and that, after careful consideration, they have reached the conclusion that this Unit, which you have done so much to foster, should now be regarded as having passed beyond the stage of experiment and should take its place as part of the ordinary organization of the Royal Air Force.

It has accordingly been decided that it should be constituted as a unit of the Royal Air Force under the orders of the Commander-in-Chief, Coastal Command, and should be commanded by a regular serving officer. Wing Commander G.W. Tuttle, DFC, has been appointed.

I am to add that the Council wish to record how much they are indebted to you for the work you have done and for the great gifts of imagination and inventive thought which you have brought to bear on the development of the technique of photography in the Royal Air Force.

It must have been a bitter moment. But in fact Cotton had already achieved the thing he had set his heart on. With the help of his devoted little team, and by his own burning conviction, his glib tongue, and his sheer brash determination to get results, he had – within the space of only nine months – laid the foundations for the triumphantly successful photographic reconnaissance of the later years of the war. In his natural role of catalyst he had 'accelerated the reactions' of everyone with whom he had dealings; at a time when accelerated reactions were extremely necessary. And although the letter he received when he landed at Heston was, in effect, an abrupt notice to quit, it should be put on record that, in the 1941 New Year's Honours List, Frederick Sidney Cotton was granted the award of Officer of the Order of the British Empire. The RAF official history of the Second World War sums up the matter thus:

Thanks to the brilliant work of a few individuals, among whom due credit must be given to the adventurous and unorthodox F.S. Cotton, there now existed a means of extensive, efficient, and economical air reconnaissance. The high-altitude Spitfires, no longer merely a promising innovation, had already become one of our most important weapons. The time was therefore ripe to bring them into line with normal Royal Air Force organization.

Even after Cotton's departure there was still the feel of adventure and pioneering at Heston, and also of ever-increasing urgency, as the threat of invasion approached. It was providential that Geoffrey Tuttle was there to take over. During his four months under Cotton he had been very definitely a second string, but when the time came for him to step into the lead he did so with marked success. There might easily have been a disastrous drop in morale after Cotton left, but Tuttle set the pace and the standards by his own inexhaustible energy and keenness. He had the good sense to accept the flying-club atmosphere, and not to try to 'regularize' the unit all at once. He was quite prepared to overlook a pilot's blue suede shoes if he was getting good photographs.

Things did gradually become more orthodox, however, and the new name which was conferred on the unit was one which no longer disguised its true function. In July 1940 it was renamed the Photographic Reconnaissance Unit, or PRU as it was usually called. But Tuttle never contemplated trying to impose any rigid orthodoxy. To his mind that would have deprived the unit of its most essential virtue: the spirit of initiative it had inherited from its originators.

It was after Tuttle took over that a new intelligence room became the centre of things at Heston; the pilots came there to be briefed and to plot their courses, and after the flight returned to tell their news to the intelligence officers. Meantime, as soon as the photographs were printed they were taken over by a team of WAAF 'plotters', whose job it was to identify the precise areas that had been covered. Working at large trestle tables in the intelligence room, they inked on to map sheets a whole series of overlapping rectangles – each representing an exposure – that looked like a pack of cards pushed over sideways. These 'plots' greatly speeded up the interpretation, for they showed at a glance the area covered by each print of the sortie.

The plotters at Heston were some of the very first WAAFs to be brought into photographic intelligence, and it had been quite a fight to get them. But both Cotton and Tuttle were convinced that women would be good at the work. Cotton once put his views on the matter in a nutshell as follows: 'My reasoning was that looking through magnifying glasses at minute objects in a photograph required the patience of Job and the skill of a good darner of socks.'

•   •   •

In July 1940 the PRU pilots were busy photographing the Dutch ports and the Channel coast; but at that time there were not yet any sinister congregations of shipping to suggest that invasion was imminent. The potential danger area had to be watched constantly, however, whatever the weather. This meant that when normal high-altitude photography was impossible owing to cloud, Tuttle had to send his pilots out on low-level sorties. The idea of photographing specific targets from below cloud had already been tried out in the days of Sidney Cotton and 'Slogger' Slocum, and this method was already known as 'dicing' – someone had once made a joke about 'dicing with death'. This special kind of photographic reconnaissance, although limited in its uses because large areas cannot be covered, is of unique value when information on a target such as shipping is urgently needed despite the weather, and Tuttle set himself to steer the development of the low-level technique. Planning was one of the secrets, because at very low levels navigation in the usual sense was not possible. The landmarks had to be memorized most carefully beforehand, for time and major landmarks were going to be the only guides.

'It's best to keep down low all the way over, so as to avoid giving an early warning to enemy radar,' Tuttle used to say, 'so you go in almost at sea-level; and you must spot your landmarks the second you see the coast. And switch on your cameras in good time before you whistle past your target. You've got to be right first time, because there isn't going to *be* a second time.' He believed that it was 'murder' to attempt the same dicing sortie twice.

Flying Officer Alistair Taylor, one of the few pilots who was a regular RAF officer, was a star performer at dicing. He was a planner *par excellence*. To Taylor's mind, preliminary planning for a 'dicer' meant not only memorizing the landmarks and calculating the time factor to the nearest second, as well as a careful study of the flak maps; it meant an intimate knowledge of all the enemy aircraft he might meet – their performance, their guns, their likely tactics.

It was always an anxious moment when a pilot was due back from dicing. Out at the edge of the tarmac as usual one cloudy afternoon in July 1940, was a blue Ford car, and beside it a solitary figure was striding up and down – Geoffrey Tuttle. He always liked to be on the spot when his pilots returned. That afternoon Alistair Taylor was out after the Dutch ports, and he was just about due back.

In the intelligence room, Flying Officer John Weaver and Pilot Officer Quentin Craig were also listening for the Spitfire when the door opened and two heads looked in: Flight Lieutenant Spencer Ring, a cool and exceedingly competent Canadian, who was commander of one of the PRU Flights, and his great friend Flying Officer 'Bill' Wise, a spirited pilot who knew what he could get away with, and habitually got away with it.

'Any gen for tomorrow yet?' asked Ring.

'Yes, Tuttle just got it from Coastal,' replied Weaver. 'Come on in.'

Ring and Wise went over to Weaver's desk and looked down the pencilled list. It was the usual thing – twenty-two top-priority jobs when there were only half a dozen

Spitfires to fly them. Meanwhile the door opened again, and an intelligence officer who was shortly coming on duty hurried in and made for Craig's telephone.

'D'you mind, Quentin, Oh, those stupid so-and-so's.'

'What's happened, Norman?' asked Craig.

Pilot Officer Sir Norman Watson, heir to an immense margarine fortune, dialled a number and waited.

'What's the point in having a Bentley, if it breaks down all the time? It gave up near Osterley, so I just left it there. Oh, hello – Watson here. That Bentley you sold me is no good at all. It's sitting by the side of the road at Osterley, so you might as well collect it. And in the meantime I shall want another; I'm completely stuck here without a motorcar. So will you send along another Bentley – *right* away.'

Wise had been listening fascinated, and at this point he edged over to Watson and gave him a nudge.

'Make it two, Norman; one for you and one for Spencer and me!'

'There he comes,' said Craig, as he heard the roar of a Merlin engine; and a few minutes later Taylor taxied up in his pale pink Spitfire (Tuttle had found that pale pink was a better colour for dicing than the usual duck-egg green).

Everyone gathered round while Taylor described his sortie. He had just finished photographing Flushing, and was starting for home, when to his horror – as he glanced around for fighters – he suddenly saw a Ju 88 only three hundred yards behind. Immediately he made a right-hand climbing turn, and then, as the German climbed after him, he just managed to give him the slip by turning sharply to the left and then beating it for the Kent coast.

This was not an exceptional encounter; it was the sort of thing that happened every day of the week as the Photographic Reconnaissance Unit got into its stride. Tuttle took great pains to ensure that the work of his pilots received recognition, and by the end of July three of them had brand new DFC ribbons: Ring, Wise, and Taylor. Gradually PRU began to build up the reputation of a secret *corps d'élite*. The story goes that later in the year a young pilot introduced his fiancée to Tuttle in the bar at Heston, and she – after a glance round the assembled company – gave the Commanding Officer the most exquisite pleasure by fastening her eyes on his purple and white ribbon and asking sweetly: 'Are those the squadron colours?'

Soon there was a waiting list of pilots who wanted to join PRU, and Tuttle could take his pick. He needed quite a lot of new men, as from July 1940 onwards there was not only Heston to think of, but the Flights at Wick in the north of Scotland and at St Eval in Cornwall. He realized how vitally important it was to choose the right pilots, for this was the moment when the pattern for the future was being set as regards flying practice. Not that he ever attempted to impose hard-and-fast methods. He firmly believed that success in photographic reconnaissance depends primarily on the individual, and he encouraged each man to work out his own variations of technique.

Perhaps one of the most important things which Tuttle did during the fourteen months he was in command of PRU was to follow through on organizing the operational training. The two main things a pilot had to be taught were to go a long way alone in a Spitfire and to fly accurately over his target. Once these elements were mastered, the first operational sortie from Heston was the Dunkirk milk-run; after that Rotterdam, and then finally Germany. The biggest risk in the early days was running out of fuel – the Spitfire used about a gallon a minute – and Tuttle found that the pilots saw at once that it was better to have fuel than guns. 'There's another reason, too, why it wouldn't make any sense for you to have guns,' he used to tell them: 'if you stopped to fight you'd be using up even more fuel. You *don't* need guns when you're flying the fastest planes in the sky.'

Tuttle expected so much, and took so much for granted, that he instilled confidence into his pilots. One young man, who was later awarded several decorations for his work in PRU, arrived at the unit very green and timid. He was greeted by a brisk enthusiastic Wing Commander Tuttle, who asked him if he'd ever flown a Spitfire. He said no, he hadn't; to which Tuttle answered, 'Well, get all the practice you can today on small single-engined types. I want you to fly one tomorrow.'

• • •

At Wembley the transition to Air Force ways was rather more complicated than at Heston, though the changes were rapid as soon as the Air Ministry decided to take over Hemming's company. Spender – still a civilian – was the leading interpreter there, and Douglas Kendall joined him after he returned from France. Meanwhile Walter Heath, with the small group of RAF and WAAF interpreters he had been training, had joined forces with the Aircraft Operating Company in April 1940, and the new joint organization was for a time known as the Photographic Development Unit (Interpretation). And to celebrate the merger, Hemming combined the initials PDU and AOC, and produced the splendid name 'Paduoc House' for the decrepit little Wembley factory.

Walter Heath's special gift was for detailed interpretation, and it was when the Germans were rushing to develop their air bases for the attack on Britain that he first began to turn his attention to airfields. He was to find that many secrets could be discovered by studying the photographs. The length of an extended runway, the size of new aircraft shelters, the installation of new night-landing equipment – all these could show unfailingly what the methodical enemy was planning. During the weeks that followed Dunkirk the intense, urgency of day-to-day reporting was paramount, however, and all hands were needed to provide information and target material for the Unit's many customers. At that stage, there was no time for detailed, long-term investigations. Nevertheless, it was the work of the few specialists at Wembley that led to the forming of specialist interpretation sections. And it was therefore in no small measure thanks to them that the whole scope of photographic intelligence was so much extended later in the war.

Such was the situation at Wembley when, at the end of June 1940, a letter which Sidney Cotton had written to the Air Ministry a few weeks before his departure had important results. Cotton had heard that Peter Riddell was leaving Bomber Command, and on the grounds that 'Squadron Leader Riddell is one of the most experienced men in the country on interpretation work', he had immediately asked if arrangements could be made to secure his services. On 26 June Riddell was posted to Wembley. Like Tuttle at Heston, he found himself the one and only regular RAF officer in a very irregular unit.

It was just the moment when an energetic organizer such as Riddell was needed; and the task which faced him was nothing less than laying the foundations for the whole future of British photographic interpretation. He plunged into the work with zest. He believed fiercely in the principle 'contract to expand', for there was still the continual risk that separate organizations would be started up. The Admiralty, the War Office, Bomber Command, were agitating all the time for photographic intelligence, and if things were even slightly wrong they were apt to jump to the conclusion that they could cope better on their own. But Riddell fought and schemed against this danger, and eventually he won. It was not merely a danger of wasteful overlapping, but a risk of disintegration – of sacrificing something too new, too unproved, too supremely valuable not to be developed in the right way.

The relationship between Wembley and the Admiralty was already on a firm footing, mainly owing to Sidney Cotton's early spadework and to the liaison between Spender and Denning. But there was not yet any proper arrangements with the War Office. When Riddell arrived he found that a wealth of the raw material for military intelligence was coming in – the photographs were bristling with guns, tanks, dumps, camps – and he pleaded with the War Office for the loan of the Army interpreters who had escaped from Dunkirk, to supervise and help with the Wembley reports. Before the end of July Walter Venour had arrived, and was soon after joined by Gerald Lacoste; but the need for a specialized Army section soon became obvious. By September the War Office had approved a new establishment, and thus an Army interpretation section started up as part of the Air Force unit – a foreshadowing of the fully-fledged inter-Service unit that was to come.

This was a time when photographic intelligence was being shaped and strengthened by an influx of outstandingly able men. One of the first, E.J. Ramsey Matthews, a very experienced cartographic surveyor, came to Wembley in May 1940 and took charge of the Wild machine and a staff of seven civilians, which freed Spender for actual interpretation. For some time Hemming had been trying to enlist the help of a former colleague, Claude Wavell, a brilliant mathematician who had taken a leading part in a pioneering air survey of Rio de Janeiro before the war. After Dunkirk Wavell telegraphed: 'If you still want me, I'll come,' and the answer flashed back: 'Come at once.' At Wembley he began by helping Douglas Kendall to start an interpretation school, and then Riddell asked him to supervise all detailed interpretation (by that time Heath was back at the Air Ministry, working entirely on airfield intelligence). But before long Wavell launched out into the field in which he became the leading British expert: the interpretation of enemy radar and 'wireless' installations.

Largely through Michael Spender, a number of men of academic distinction were drawn in: he maintained right from the start that their sort of work was a good background for interpretation. Two of the earliest arrivals were 'Bill' Wager, now Professor of Geology at Oxford, and Glyn Daniel, the Cambridge archaeologist whose cheery likeable informality and knack of exposition have become known to millions since the war through the television programme *Animal, Vegetable, Mineral?* Within a few weeks, Pilot Officers Wager and Daniel were in charge of interpretation shifts, and could help to ease the load on Spender and Kendall. Other valuable additions to the team at Wembley were Alfred Stephenson, a polar explorer, who later directed all interpretation training; and David Linton, an expert geographer (now Professor of Geography at Sheffield).

Then in the early autumn of 1940 there turned up at Wembley a quiet elderly officer named Flight Lieutenant Hamshaw Thomas, the very man who had been one of the stalwarts of photographic interpretation in the First World War. Ever since the outbreak of the Second World War, when he left his work as a botonist at Cambridge to join the RAF, he had been trying to get back to interpretation, but he had been tossed hither and thither by the vicissitudes of postings, and it took him almost a year before he finally managed to reach Wembley. He was longing to revise the Air Ministry's manual of interpretation, which was seriously out of date, and Riddell set him to work on this at once. The analysis of industry particularly interested him, and he soon began to concentrate on factories and the clues to their activity. This interest of his shortly led to the formation of an Industry Section, which throughout the rest of the war produced a wealth of valuable reports. It may seem a far cry from the study of fossil plants, which is Hamshaw Thomas's special subject, to the interpretation of Nazi war industry;

but it is the same patient approach and deductive reasoning that brings success in both. Some time after the Industry Section got going, Douglas Kendall was helping to escort Field-Marshal Smuts round the interpretation unit, and Hamshaw Thomas was called upon to show the Field-Marshal his work. Smuts was tremendously interested and impressed, and also much pleased to see Hamshaw Thomas again, as he had known him years earlier. Afterwards, his comment to Kendall was: 'D'you know, that man's one of the best botonists in the world.'

After a month at Wembley, Riddell drew up his blue-print. It was a masterly synthesis of the methods he had himself tried and proved at Bomber Command, and of various practices that had been introduced at Wembley and Heston under Sidney Cotton. In it he formulated the pattern that was later followed out in the vast machinery of the Allied Central Interpretation Unit.

One of the most important principles he defined was that there should be three successive stages of interpretation, or 'Phases' as they were named.

'First Phase' meant immediate reporting of important news items: the movements of ships and aircraft, of rail traffic and canal traffic; the extent of bomb damage, and the position of ammunition dumps. In cases of special urgency this information was to be available three hours after the aircraft landed. 'Second Phase' reports were to be out within twenty-four hours, and they were to give not only quite a lot of detail on general activity but also, by dealing with a day's accumulation of cover, a coordinated view of what was going on. The 'Third Phase' report, to be issued later, were to be very detailed statements for specialist recipients, on such things as airfields, factories, and military installations.

In the summer of 1940, when everyone was demanding immediate information, it would have been easy to ignore everything else and concentrate entirely on

First Phase. But Riddell had the grasp and foresight to see that the photographs held infinitely more than snap answers, and he planned accordingly.

Originally all the interpretation was done at Wembley, but within a few months there were First Phase sections at Wick and St Eval as well as at Heston; so that almost as soon as the films were processed the Admiralty and Air Ministry had teleprint statements on activity at the ports and anchorages of southern Norway and western France, as well as the supremely important news of what was happening across the Channel.

• • •

All through the summer of 1940 the interpretation unit at Wembley watched the invasion ports like a cat watching a whole series of rat-holes; but still the rat – in the form of an assembling invasion fleet – did not put in an appearance.

Many very significant things were, however, going on along the French coast, and they were watched and reported day by day. As early as July, new photographs of Cap Gris Nez sounded off an alarm, for the tidy patchwork of little fields that reaches almost to the cliffs had lost its normal look of peace and quiet. There was a network of newly trodden paths, and the beginnings of three huge pits, each twice as large as a house. The freshly exposed earth showed up a glaring photographic white against the calm greys of the natural landscape, and the whole thing had the look of new military construction – an unmistakable look of violation like hobnailed footprints on snow. Within a month the first of the great 12-inch guns was in position, and the War Office, which in May had formed a department for receiving photographic intelligence, pressed for more frequent covers and eagerly awaited the interpretations.

Venour and Lacoste and the other interpreters did their

utmost to keep pace with the system of defences that the Germans were putting up along the French coast; and there was much to report besides guns. Round St Omer, for example, new telephone lines – betrayed by the shadow of each post and the pale circle of newly turned earth at its foot – indicated where local headquarters were installed. And five miles inland from Calais the myriad tracks of heavy lorries converging on the Forêt de Guines left no doubt as to where ammunition and stores for the invasion were being hidden.

At the fighter bases in the Pas-de-Calais, and the bomber bases further afield, there was so much of importance to report that in August a Third Phase airfield section was started at Wembley, headed by a WAAF interpreter, Flight Officer Hammerton, who had been trained by Walter Heath.

While the stage was being set on the French coast, the landing craft without which the invasion could not begin were being hurriedly prepared in the shipyards of the Low Countries. In July, Michael Spender found that five 130-ft barges at Rotterdam had modified bows, presumably for the landing of tanks and troops, but because of the small scale of the photographs he could say no more. By mid August, however, Wembley could report that at Antwerp, at Rotterdam, and at Amsterdam, the fleet of makeshift invasion craft lay ready. When would it start to move?

On 29 August, and again two days later, came the earliest warnings – the chilly gusts of wind before the first drops of rain. The news was negative, but nonetheless definite: fifty-six barges had disappeared from Amsterdam. Two days later a hundred more had left Antwerp. Then late on 31 August, eighteen of them were photographed at Ostend, and during the next six days and nights the procession gathered in volume: by 6 September two hundred barges were assembled in the harbour.

Each new cover of Boulogne, Calais, and Dunkirk confirmed that the enemy was moving into position to strike, in spite of presenting such close-range targets to the British bombers. On the day that the country was warned of 'Imminent Invasion' Spender and Kendall and their interpreters counted feverishly, and Peter Riddell hardly left the telephone. Those rows of patched up barges, huddled side by side with their bows to the quay for loading, seemed sinister enough at the time, but looking back at the photographs now, they suggest – most incongruously – litter after litter of gigantic piebald piglets nuzzling at the sides of the quays.

For the next ten days the tension mounted as the numbers of barges steadily increased at the ports nearest to Britain, and were joined by crowds of E-boats and other small craft. The Heston Spitfires brought back photographs of the supply bases as well as of the Channel ports, and both at Hamburg and at Antwerp there were assemblies of merchant vessels waiting to move forward. They also brought pictures of convoys of barges on the move down the coast, in formations so tidy that it was clear the German Navy was in charge.

The climax came on 17 September, when there were 266 barges at Calais, 220 at Dunkirk, 205 at Le Havre, 230 at Boulogne, 200 at Ostend, and 600 at Antwerp. That night, in Secret Session, the Prime Minister told Parliament: 'At any moment a major assault may be launched upon this Island. I now say in secret that upwards of 1,700 self-propelled barges and more than 200 sea-going ships, some very large ships, are already gathered at the many invasion ports in German occupation.'

While Churchill spoke, Spender was re-checking the number of barges at Dunkirk – 130 had arrived in four days. Suddenly he sprang to his feet an threw down his stereoscope.

'We don't want these,' he exclaimed. 'They'd better give us rifles!'

The suspense continued for another few days. The

armada was poised, ready to strike, and the quays of the Channel ports were swarming with activity. But meanwhile the Battle of Britain had been fought and won, and the Luftwaffe had failed to gain air supremacy. We know now that Hitler had already decided to abandon 'Sea Lion'.

The armada still remained poised, but nevertheless the new photographs showed something very significant. The Wembley interpreters were already learning that nothing ever happens without leaving a track, or evidence of some kind, even if the evidence is negative. The first sign that the crisis had passed was an indefinable change in the look of the quays. At first it was indefinable, but soon there was a very clear slacking off of activity. And then as October came, and as the interpreters checked and re-checked their barge totals, it became certain that the invasion fleet was beginning to disperse. The piebald piglets were shifted, and docked side by side parallel to the quays – the normal position for commercial barges – and then those that had not been bombed to bits gradually slipped away up the coast. The danger of invasion was past.

●　　●　　●

There was one day in the summer of 1940 when the unrelenting hard work was set aside both at Heston and Wembley: the day when the King and Queen made a formal visit of inspection. At Wembley there was a brave display of RAF uniforms: Wing Commander Hemming escorted the King; Squadron Leader Riddell accompanied the Queen; and Michael Spender appeared for the first time as a Flight Lieutenant. Afterwards Hemming was asked why there had been such a lot of merriment when the royal party reached the maps and charts.

'Oh well,' chuckled Hemming, 'how was the King to know that the word "Wild" means something special for us, and that we pronounce it "Vilt"? When he saw those big folders marked WILD PLANS, he burst out laughing and said to me, "You wouldn't like to show me what's in those, would you?"'

Two months later the hut where the Wild plans were kept was a roofless wreck, and at the entrance of the shelter next to it an airman had been killed. On 2 October 1940, in the early hours of the morning, the interpretation unit received a direct hit from an oil bomb. Again a fortnight later, 'Paduoc House' was almost blasted down. After this the roof was no longer at all weatherproof, and the Third Phase interpreters upstairs often had to wear raincoats and put up umbrellas over their desks. A search began for more suitable quarters; but throughout the winter of the Blitz the work went on at Wembley, to the accompaniment of sirens and bombs and guns, and the endless shunting of the trains in the railway yards across the way.

The bombing at Heston was much more severe than at Wembley, and in the third week of September things began to get quite bad. On the Thursday night an enemy bomber went throbbing overhead, but apparently did not drop anything. Five minutes later, however, there was a terrific explosion outside the main hangar. A magnetic mine had been dropped by parachute, and the hangar was a flattened mess of twisted girders. Crushed beneath the debris were five precious Spitfires and also the famous Lockheed G-AFTL.

A few days later Geoffrey Tuttle was working in his office, which was by this time in a somewhat rickety state, when the Adjutant, Flight Lieutenant Noel Sherwell, came to him with an incredulous expression on his face.

'The guard says the King is waiting at the gate,' he announced, 'and he wants to see you.'

Tuttle, equally unbelieving, came to the gate with Sherwell to see what trick someone was playing. But there sure enough was a genuine royal car, and inside it was HM King George VI. Tuttle snapped to attention with a smart salute, and His Majesty smiled and explained.

'I was driving from Windsor to London and I happened to look out towards Heston, and suddenly I realised that the big hangar wasn't there any more. So I just called in to see how you were all getting on.'

In the second half of October, when the Blitz began in earnest, Heston got night after night of high explosive and incendiaries. The photographic processing section was the worst hit: three times it was 'dispersed' to quarters outside the airfield, and three times it was hit again. Tuttle insisted that the pilots must get some proper sleep, so he took a house for them at Cookham; but he himself did not leave his post. At this time he had no deputy. He used to look in at Shelter 'H', where the night-shift plotters were working, and where Quentin Craig's dog snapped at an occasional rat; and then he would sit alone in the Officers' Mess and wait for the bombers. Sometimes he managed to snatch a little sleep, and sometimes he turned on the radio-gramophone and played Ravel's *Bolero* over and over again.

In the daytime the flying went on at an increasing tempo, and at the end of October an 'extra-super-long-range' Spitfire was ready for action. It was so heavily loaded with fuel that it was nicknamed 'the bowser'. Flying Officer S.J. Millen (who was killed only two months later on a dicing sortie) was the pilot who achieved the first great success in it, when he made the longest sortie yet flown by PRU. He was out for five hours and twenty minutes, and came back with photographs of Stettin and Rostock – the first and long-awaited cover of the Baltic coast. Just a week later Flight Lieutenant P. Corbishley flew 'the bowser' southwards to photograph Marseilles and Toulon, and both pilots were awarded DFCs.

But although at Heston, as at Wembley, the work went on in spite of the Blitz, there had clearly got to be a move – the sooner the better – and on Boxing Day 1940 the whole unit packed its bags and started to move to Benson, the Oxfordshire airfield that was to be its home for the rest of the war.

• • •

Across the road from 'Paduoc House' there was a row of little mock-Tudor villas, shabby and draughty from the bombing, and in one of these, for fifteen shivering days from 1 December 1940, five WAAFs and one rather embarrassed young Army officer applied themselves to learning how to interpret aerial photographs. I was one of the WAAFs.

We sat in our greatcoats in a sparsely furnished upstairs room, and took down notes while Douglas Kendall, in his quiet emphatic way, kindled our interest in the dimensions and armament of German battleships, and chalked up one after another the plan views of the Channel ports. I was amazed that he knew them all by heart.

For our first exercise we were given some 'verticals' (photographs taken from vertically above), and we gradually learnt how to recognize such major landmarks as railway stations and airfields, and to distinguish between railways, with their invariable gentle curves, and roads, which usually follow the lie of the land.

There are always shadows on daytime high-altitude photographs, because the pictures could not have been taken except from a clear sky; and I learnt how much easier it is to look at the prints if you place them with the shadows falling towards you; as though the sun were shining down on the photograph from beyond the table you're working at. We could have done with some sunshine in that freezing room, where the sputtering gas fire seemed to give out more noise than heat.

Shipping was of course the first priority, and we practised making accurate counts, listing the vessels by size – large, medium, and small. We didn't yet know enough about recognition points to identify many types.

I myself was much looking forward to seeing more German aircraft, because I was intensely keen about aviation and had been writing for *The Aeroplane* for some years before the war. But the first aerial photograph of an enemy airfield I ever saw was a disappointment and shock. It was a busy fighter base in the Pas-de-Calais, and I had to try and count the aircraft; but even under a magnifying glass the Me 109s were no bigger than pin-heads, in fact rather smaller. My heart sank, and I thought, 'I shall never be able to do this.' A bit later, however, we had an aircraft test which was more to my taste: we were given some good clear photographs of a dump of French aircraft which the Germans had written off at Merignac, near Bordeaux, and had to identify as many as we could, with the help of some recognition silhouettes. I thoroughly enjoyed myself, but was rather worried because when I took my list to Kendall there was one aeroplane I hadn't been able to name. Kendall smiled. 'No,' he said. 'Nor can I.'

We started by looking at single prints, but were soon trying to use a stereoscope, that apparently simple optical instrument which presents exaggerated height and depth – if the 'pair' of photographs below it is set in just the right position. There were not enough stereoscopes to go round, and I realized that a 'stereo' was something important and precious. In time I borrowed one. It was an absurdly uncomplicated little gadget, like a pair of spectacles mounted in a single rectangular piece of metal, supported by four metal legs that held it a few inches above the photographs. I stood it above a pair of prints as I had seen some of the others doing. I could see two images, not one, and there really did not seem much point. It was much simpler to work with an ordinary magnifying glass. I edged the two prints backwards and forwards a bit – still two images; and then suddenly the thing happened, the images fused, and the buildings in the photograph shot up towards me so that I almost drew back. It was the same sort of feeling of triumph and wonder that I remember long ago when I first stayed up on a bicycle without someone holding on behind. From then on interpretation was much easier.

Towards the end of the fortnight, Michael Spender came and gave us a talk about the interpretation of shipping. In his hesitant but intimidating voice he spoke of the principles that apply to all interpretation.

'You must know at a glance what is normal, and then you can recognize the abnormal when you see it. When we saw the Dutch shipyards crowded with barges having their bows cut away, we knew the importance of what was happening because we had already been watching the normal life of those yards. And because we knew the normal look of the Channel ports we could recognize the abnormal the moment the barges started appearing there. An interpreter is like a motorist driving through a town, who suddenly sees a rubber ball bouncing across the road from a side street. He can't see any children playing, but he knows in a flash they are there and his brake is on. You must know what is normal, but you must also know the significance of what you see when you see it.'

We listened enthralled to this farouche Flight Lieutenant, who knew so much and expected so much; but his wonderful ideas did not really seem to bear much relation to our little exercises of counting and identifying.

The climax of the course, on which our fate depended, was an oral examination by Peter Riddell. We were much in awe of the dark, busy Squadron Leader who looked in occasionally for a quick word with Kendall. We knew that he couldn't tolerate inefficiency, and we trembled as we thought how inefficient we were.

The night before the exam I sat on my bed in my Wembley billet, forgetful of the thud of bombs, and went over and over the silhouette – *Bismarck*, *Tirpitz*, *Prinz Eugen* . . . shipping was my weakest subject. And then finally I consoled myself by reading a letter which had just come from a trusted friend in the RAF.

I haven't the least doubt that you will sail through your present course with flying colours – but if, by some fickle chance, things don't go quite as you had hoped, don't take it too hardly. I am told that photographic interpretation requires a peculiar mentality – a kind of super jig-saw mind – which bears no relation to brains or ability.

Well, by the next evening it would be all over.

The following afternoon Riddell appeared without any ceremony and sat on a table while he shot questions at us. 'How do you tell the difference between a naval unit and a merchant vessel?' he asked me.

I was paralysed – oh, why hadn't he asked me the wing-span of a German aeroplane? He turned to my neighbour, Eve Holiday, and asked gently: 'Do *you* know?' Eve did know and had been waiting eagerly.

'A merchant vessel is like an oblong box with pointed ends, and a naval unit is a very elongated oval – *cigar shaped*.' She drew a cigar shape in the air to stress her point. Oh yes, of course, I know quite well really.

Next it was the turn of a WAAF with a long little face and the fragile look of a wild flower – Ann McKnight-Kauffer, daughter of the famous poster artist. 'In the German Army are there more mechanized divisions or horse-drawn?' Riddell asked her.

It was rather a catch question, and Ann was caught. 'M-m-mechanized, I think,' she replied.

And so it went on. We were certain we had all failed. But in fact that fifth training course at Wembley was the first on which every one of the candidates got through.

So it was in January 1941 that I took my place on one of the Second Phase shifts, twelve hours on and twenty-four hours off alternately. Wearing my new uniform with the almost invisible thin stripe of an Assistant Section Officer, I worked alongside a kind and cheerful Australian WAAF officer called Jean Starling. I had to tackle shipping quite often, but as all the others preferred it, and I much preferred aircraft, I more often got the airfields.

As a result of the Air Ministry's keen interest in enemy airfields, major changes had to be reported by Second Phase, as well as by the Third Phase airfield section. I was rather taken aback, however, to find that the aircraft themselves were normally reported rather as an afterthought, at the end of the statement on the airfield itself. Surely this was putting the cart before the horse – or rather the stage before the play that was being acted? But it was hardly for a WAAF who had been an officer only a few weeks to say so.

During the times when reconnaissance was held up by weather I used every spare moment to add to my knowledge of aircraft. I thought that before long I might be asked to interpret Italian aircraft, and I knew practically nothing about them. So I spent hours with *Jane's All the World's Aircraft*, and set down the main things I thought important. One of the civilian interpreters who had been with the Aircraft Operating Company, Ray Herschel, was interested in aircraft too; and I picked up from him how to link the facts in *Jane's* with the tiny shapes on the photographs.

In a few short weeks my notes on Italian aircraft were turning into a sort of report, and when it was finished I was told, much to my surprise, that Squadron Leader Riddell wanted to see it. The next morning he sent for me and I felt a bit apprehensive. Could I have made some dreadful boob?

I went towards his office, but he happened to be in the passage outside, with my report in his hand.

'I've looked through this,' he said. 'Aircraft are extremely important, and they ought to be reported in more detail. Would you like to start an aircraft interpretation section?'

FOUR

THE START OF THE BOMBING

It was just six months after war was declared, on the night of 19 March 1940, that the RAF made its first bombing attack against a target on German ground. For Bomber Command this was a long-awaited occasion: the first chance to show what it could really do.

At the RAF Station at Hemswell in Lincolnshire, in the early hours of the following morning, two intelligence officers sat waiting while the hands of the clock crawled on. There was nothing you could do but wait. Hours ago the intelligence room had been full of eager young men: the pilots and aircrews who had gathered round while Squadron Leader Browne and Flight Lieutenant Hamshaw Thomas pointed out on the map the long thin shape of the island of Sylt, and explained that the sea-plane station at Hornum was one of the main bases used by the German mine-laying aircraft which were being such a serious threat to British shipping in the North Sea. Then Air Vice-Marshal Arthur Harris himself, at that time in command of No. 5 Bomber Group, came in to give his aggressive encouragement; and when the boys trooped out they were keyed up for an attack that was going to make history.

A total of 49 bombers were taking part: Wellingtons, Whitleys, and Hampdens. The last of the Hampdens had roared off into the darkness a very long time ago, so it seemed to Henshaw Thomas; and much had happened elsewhere since then.

At midnight the House of Commons, toiling in late session, had burst into cheers when the Prime Minister, Neville Chamberlain, announced that the recent German air-raid on Scapa Flow was being richly avenged; that even while he spoke British bombs were obliterating the main enemy air base at Sylt. He explained that the news had come 400 miles over the North Sea from the landing aircraft while it was still directing the attack. The message had been decoded and sent straight on to him, so that he could announce the news while the raid was still in progress. It was an event 'probably without precedent in the history of warfare'.

At Hemswell, Browne kept glancing at the clock, and listening for the first sound of homecoming aircraft. Very soon now. And at any moment Harris would be over again from Waddington, the other 5 Group airfield from which bombers had been sent out. Hamshaw Thomas knocked out his ancient pipe and then refilled it, but it wouldn't light properly, and he had to start all over again.

When the bombers did get back the interrogation went on for hours, and in the chilly silence before daybreak, after Hamshaw Thomas had finished helping Browne to make out the returns for Group headquarters, he thought back over what the crews had said. It had been courageous of those boys to stick to their stories of what actually happened, even though it wasn't as dramatic as Harris would have liked. Still, the raid had been a wonderful success; just what the bomber crews needed to boost their morale – and the country too. 'I wonder what the paper will make of it,' thought Hamshaw Thomas, as he had a bite of breakfast before going off to bed.

The papers were in no doubt at all what to make of it. The headlines blazed out: LAND TARGET AT LAST FOR THE RAF – TONS OF BOMBS DROPPED – SIX HOURS' ATTACK ON SYLT – HANGARS AND OIL TANKS ABLAZE – ADMIRATION IN

US – NIGHT SKY LIT UP. The British Press also exposed the subtleties of German propaganda, and held up to ridicule certain insinuations which arrived via Rotterdam. GERMANY CHANGES THE SUBJECT – 'HAIL OF BOMBS' ON DENMARK – ran the headlines on the Foreign News page of *The Times*, and the report went on to claim:

> The best proof that last night's raid of the RAF on Sylt was an effective enterprise can be seen in the fact that the Nazis are diverting attention from the raid to the unintentional violation of Danish neutrality by some of the British aircraft. They contrive to convey the impression that the main British raid was not on the German island but on Denmark.

While the British public gloated, the headquarters of Bomber Command was filled with incredulous elation. After six dreary months of impotence and failure, here at last was the turning of the tide. The crowning confirmation of this great success would be photographs of the damage taken the day after the raid; and almost as soon as the last of the bombers landed, two photographic Blenheims went off to get pictures.

That evening Peter Riddell waited impatiently in the photographic intelligence section of Bomber Command's headquarters, a cosy underground chamber dominated by a vast wall-map of Germany stuck full of target flags. The Blenheims had returned safely all right, but the films had to be processed and brought over to High Wycombe. The photographic section at Bomber Command was all set to turn out special enlargements – lots of them; the press was clamouring for pictures.

Riddell's interpreters all wanted to have a hand in this triumphant occasion, and the six of them sat round waiting. There was A.P.F. Fane, famous before the war as a racing driver – he later did brilliant work as a photographic pilot; and the three other RAF officers were

Eric Fuller, whose knowledge of the lay-out of industrial plants was very useful, Tom Muir Warden, a Canadian who had become interested in aerial photographs in connection with his work as a mining engineer, and 'Schloss' Windsor, so nicknamed by Fane immediately he arrived, who had previously been in the aerial photography business. The two civilians, who later became WAAF officers, were a blonde and a brunette, Cynthia Wood and Angus Wilson – both of them talented interpreters.

Riddell was smoking cigarette after cigarette, and Fane was playing about with a loaded revolver, as he often did (he was a crack shot), while Fuller was trying to read an intelligence report, and the others were pretending to work. Fuller looked up and broke the silence.

'Where's Stolp?'

There was a shattering explosion and the girls screamed. An officer and several airmen came running in from the photographic section next door to see what had happened, and they found Fane laughing and the rest of the section speechless. In the huge wall map of Germany there was a neat round hole above the name 'Stolp'.

At last a sergeant hurried in with a packet of photographs, and Riddell grabbed them and divided up the prints among his team. For a long time not a word was spoken. There was not even a sound from Fane, who was wont to burst into song when the work was not specially urgent. Then one by one the interpreters took their prints over to Riddell. They were not very clear photographs, but clear enough to tell their unmistakable news. Below his stereoscope Riddell could see the Hornum hangars looking as boxlike as ever, and the Heinkel float-planes sitting about as usual on the slipway, and the oil tanks solidly intact – unquestionably, horribly intact. A sickening sinking feeling took hold of him, and his first thought was 'There must be a mistake; these must be some old photographs taken before the raid.' He looked at the date strip. No, 20 March.

Then with grim decision he told the interpreters: 'We must find out where the bombs *did* go.'

Deep despondency settled on the section as all through the night they searched the Sylt sand-dunes, hoping and longing to find *something* to show that bombs had fallen on the island. But by morning there were less than half a dozen rings drawn in chinagraph pencil to mark the findings: a handful of possible craters among the dunes, and a tiny hole in the roof of one of the hangars at Hornum.

Bright and early the telephone rang. Riddell answered, and it was the Senior Air Staff Officer, Air Vice-Marshal Norman Bottomley, sounding very cheerful.

'Have you shaved yet?'

'Yes, I have sir.'

'Well, you'd better get into your best uniform quick, as you've got to go to Buckingham Palace with some Sylt enlargements.'

There was a moment's pause, and then Riddell said: 'Can I see you in your office first, sir? It's rather important.'

A few minutes later he was back. 'All the photographs,' he said, 'right away. I'm going to show them to Ludlow. You all stay here. No one must know at the moment. I'd better lock the door.' He gathered up the prints like a pack of cards, snatched a map of Sylt, and hurried off to the Commander-in-Chief's office.

'It can't be true,' said Ludlow-Hewitt. 'You must show me; I must see with my own eyes.'

Riddell spread out the map on the floor, and then the photographs beside it, and Ludlow-Hewitt went over to the door and turned the key.

'Here, sir,' pointed out Riddell, on his hands and knees. 'This is all we've been able to find. We've been at it all night.'

Ludlow-Hewitt knelt beside him and examined the photographs through a magnifying glass. After a few minutes he had seen enough.

'I must tell Newall.'

'Would you like me to go out, sir?' asked Riddell.

Ludlow-Hewitt sighed. 'No, you stay.' He reached for his telephone. 'Get me the Chief of the Air Staff,' he said.

On the evening of 22 March 1940, the Air Ministry issued the following announcement to the Press:

> RAF aircraft carried out a reconnaissance on the island of Sylt on Wednesday morning with a view to confirming the results of the previous night's attack. The photographs taken have proved to be of no value in indicating the extent of the material damage inflicted in the course of the heavy attack.

In the meantime, the Germans hastened to invite various neutral journalists to visit Sylt. But so strong was wishful thinking in England that their reports cut no ice with the British Press and public, and it was happily believed that labour gangs had been put to work so effectively in filling up craters and repairing damage that the reporters had been completely taken in.

Within a few weeks, however, the rights and wrongs of what had happened at Sylt were forgotten as Europe staggered under the onrush of German invasions – first Denmark and Norway; then Holland, Belgium, France. But from the viewpoint of the relationship between bombing and photographic intelligence, the story of the 'successful' attack on Sylt and the photographs that could not lie stands as a permanent landmark.

●　　●　　●

Looking back after seventeen years, it is all too easy to blame and criticize, and mock. But to see the Sylt incident in proper perspective one must look back further still, to the years between the wars; to a period when an obsessive fear of bombing was growing up.

Ever since the Zeppelin raids, bombardment from the air had been a haunting terror; and the theory of bombing had been developed to such an extent, not only by peacetime strategists but by the press and by writers of science-fiction, that the idea of it evoked the same sort of fear that the idea of nuclear warfare does at the present day. In 1938 Professor J.B.S. Haldane came out with some terrifying figures based on the effects of bombing in the Spanish war. He estimated that 20,000 people would be killed each time there was a mass attack by 500 aeroplanes, if each were carrying two tons of bombs. But hypothetical statistics such as these bore very little relation to the actual capabilities of the aircraft and bombs of the time. Nevertheless, the views summed up in Baldwin's dictum, 'the bomber will always get through', led most people to believe that bombing raids would unfailingly achieve their aims, in spite of anti-aircraft defences, and adverse weather, and human fallibility. And once the 'success' of the attack on Sylt had been so loudly proclaimed there was no going back. Inevitably there were frequent discrepancies between the published stories of bombing triumphs and the reality of what was actually happening as the British bomber force struggled into life by the hardest of ways.

There were some genuine successes of course, and when photographs did confirm spectacular destruction, such as the breaching of the Dortmund-Ems canal in the summer of 1940, and the smashing up of invasion barges at the Channel ports, the most striking pictures were released to the press and gave everyone an encouraging feeling of confidence in the high standards of British bombing.

But although 'the photographs' were sometimes useful as propaganda, the whole subject of photographic reconnaissance was a painful one at Bomber Command in these early days. Quite aside from the disappointing facts that the interpreters often brought to light, the high casualty rate of the Blenheims was a constant nightmare;

and as 1940 wore on it seemed more and more imperative that the Command should have its own photographic Spitfires. Ludlow-Hewitt had begun to press for this after Cotton's cover of the Ruhr, but it was not until nearly the end of the year, at a time when policy was being readjusted after the immediate threat of invasion was past, that the project was at last agreed to by the Air Ministry. In November 1940, Bomber Command started up its own Photographic Reconnaissance Unit.

A few miles from Cambridge, in the flat open country at the edge of the fens, lies RAF Station Oakington; and it was there that No. 3 PRU came into being. It was fated to a strange mixture of failure and success, for its primary aim – to operate photographic Spitfires *independently* for purposes of damage assessment – was abandoned within eight months; but its secondary job, the development of night reconnaissance by means of flash bombs, led unexpectedly to the evolution of a new and undreamt-of science: the detailed interpretation of the photographs taken by the night bombers themselves. It was the evidence of these night photographs, more than any other single factor, that eventually forced into view the desperate need for new navigational methods.

The bombers of the day – Hampdens, Wellingtons, and Whitleys – had from the first been provided with cameras, so that they could bring back a record of where their bombs went down on the daylight raids. Then when the British bombers proved defenceless against the onslaught of enemy fighters, and turned to night operations, the camera experts at Bomber Command and at the Royal Aircraft Establishment at Farnborough set themselves to work out plans for using flashlight techniques operationally. But the whole business was exceptionally tricky. The camera had to be synchronized both with the dropping of the bombs and with the explosion of the flash bomb, which was supposed to go off at exactly the right moment on its way to the ground. And from the viewpoint of the bomber crews, the handling of the flash bomb was a very awkward extra. Nevertheless, during 1940 a few aircraft were equipped, and by the time the new unit at Oakington started, some two hundred operational night photographs had been taken.

The man who gave the impetus to the experimental interpretation of night photographs was Squadron Leader P.B.B. Ogilvie, an exuberant young Scotsman who had been put in command of 3 PRU; and the other leading pioneer was one of his close friends, my own brother Bernard.

Pat Ogilvie had for some time been a well-known figure at Bomber Command, and everyone at the headquarters knew of his enthusiasm for aerial photography, his sudden brainwaves, and his unconventional ways. He was undoubtedly a live wire and just the man to lead the new unit. It was a job after Pat's heart; new, exciting, important, full of danger. He would get lots of operational flying, but he could also press on with all the development work that needed doing so badly. He could follow up the experiments he had been making in night reconnaissance, and could still keep in touch with Farnborough, working out ideas for improving scale and quality.

But he needed the right people for his team. He already had some good pilots lined up to fly the Spitfires, and Eric Fuller was coming from Bomber Command as intelligence officer; but he had to find someone to help with plotting the daylight sorties, and also to sort out and analyse the statistics on the performance of the night cameras – someone with an instinct for mathematics and a trained mind. Bernard Babington Smith was the man he wanted. Pat knew he had joined the Air Force and was just finishing his officers' training course.

Pat and my brother had been friends for years. They were both keen athletes, and had kept in touch although they struck out along very different lines – Bernard as a teacher of psychology at St Andrews University, and Pat first of all as a research botanist (when he became an expert photographer), and then as a traveller in soap. Finally Pat joined the RAF as a regular, and soon began to specialize in photography.

On 1 December 1940, Pilot Officer Babington Smith arrived at Oakington. Pat had volunteered to try and find somewhere for the Ogilvies, the Babington Smiths, and the Fullers to live, and he went to a house agent in Cambridge and asked for twelve bedrooms and a ghost. The agent said he couldn't manage a ghost, but there was a manor house at Coton with a water system which he thought would do instead. So the three families joined forces at Coton Manor, and each day Bernard and Pat and Eric Fuller drove along the country lanes to Oakington; and each day Bernard found himself drawn more deeply into the fascination of the strange new world of aerial photography.

His work at first consisted almost entirely of plotting the damage assessment sorties, and in the process of this he acquired the habit of keeping simultaneously in mind the two questions: 'Where has the pilot been?' and 'What has he photographed?' But soon Pat had him working on night photographs as well. It had been arranged for copies of all the operational night photographs to be sent to Pat at Oakington, and there was quite a stack of them piling up. Bernard had never set eyes on a night photograph before, but as soon as Pat explained the idea, his interest was kindled.

'The first thing is to try and find out where the chap's been, and the only proof of this is if you can plot the photograph exactly. The Stations have been making their reports, but the whole thing needs proper coordinating. And then, if you can plot the photograph, and if it was taken at the right moment to show the bomb bursts, you can report where the bombs fell, and this can be linked up with the damage assessment sorties by the interpreters at Bomber Command. It's all at an experimental stage really, but it's pretty exciting.'

So Bernard gradually learnt how to work on both day and night photographs, and little by little the appearance of the regions of north-west Europe, seen from far above, became as familiar to him as the roads and lanes between Oakington and Coton. Later in the war, when he was head of a large section devoted to the interpretation of night photographs, he used to teach his people that the way to become good at plotting was to learn the face of the land. Not just the map of Europe, but the actual face and features of the land: the polders in Holland, where the newer dykes have been laid out in regular patterns, and the older ones tend to follow some natural feature in the lie of the land; the curious narrow fields near Hamburg; the irregular fields and woods near Kiel, pockmarked with pools and mounds; the intense cultivation around Cologne; the patchwork quilt of Brittany. If you keep on looking at more and more photographs with an eye for this sort of thing, you will one day perhaps be able to pick up a night photograph with a greyish blur of crossroads, or a wood and a few fields, and say 'That's probably near Bremen', or even 'That's near Bremen', before ever taking a look at a map. Such certainty as this can be attained in time if, after a flight is over, the facts are before you, recorded in photographic form. But it is an entirely different matter for a navigator who has to try and identify landmarks in the dim moonlight far below while the flight is actually in progress. Even the most superhumanly alert and conscientious navigator could never give the same sort of answer; and indeed his prime responsibility of steering a course means that the subconscious question in his mind is, 'How far have we got on our course?' rather than 'Where are we?' So if evasive action has had to be taken, or the winds have been unexpectedly strong and the aircraft has got off her course, the chances that a river, any river, or a town, any town, will be mistaken for the river or town that 'ought' to be there are very great indeed.

At the end of 1940, the fact that there was a high percentage of serious discrepancies between the claims of the crews and the evidence of the night photographs had not yet been realized by anyone. But all through the winter, as a steady trickle of operational photographs kept arriving at Oakington, and Bernard continued examining them and recording his findings – with keen encouragement from Pat – the hard facts began to emerge.

When the statistics for three whole months had been compiled, a summary of them was sent to Bomber Command. It showed that out of the 151 flashlight photographs that had been attempted in three months by the bombers of Nos. 3 and 5 Groups, not more than 21 showed the target area. And in one case a crew had estimated its position as within fifty miles of a certain pinpoint when in fact it was a hundred miles further east.

To Pat and Bernard, these facts and figures were heart-rendering, chiefly because they seemed to show that Bomber Command was concerned with the wrong issue. The reason the photographs were being taken was to help with damage assessment, but their value was much higher in bringing to light errors of navigation. The crews were being asked to do the absolutely impossible; to navigate accurately from almost double the heights they had been trained at; heights to which they were forced up by anti-aircraft fire, and from which a momentary glimpse of a river winding far below might just as well be the Meuse as the Rhine.

The urgency of the need to improve matters would not be realized unless the whole painful situation were brought to light; but it was hardly to be expected that everyone would take this objective view. During the spring of 1941, as the stark facts began to be known throughout Bomber Command, various people reacted in various ways. The intelligence officers who were the first to see the bombers' night photographs had to decide whether to draw attention to failures of navigation, and it was not an easy decision.

Some of the crews who were told of their errors frankly disbelieved the photographs; while others took them very seriously and got worried and depressed.

Perhaps it is hardly surprising that night photography was not very popular with the crews. Although some of the men were only too pleased to be able to check their results with a view to doing better next time, others felt strongly that they had quite enough to do, and enough risks to take, without learning a lot of extra drill (not to mention carting about a whacking great cylinder which might explode at the wrong moment), and filling in a lot of extra forms, and having to fly straight and level when they ought to be weaving. And what was it all in aid of? You might just as well have a malicious snooper on board, to tell tales to the intelligence officers if everything hadn't gone right.

At higher levels also there were some who could not bring themselves to face the facts, and others who faced them and were deeply disturbed. At one Group headquarters, the intelligence officers found it was best not to say anything about the photographs which did not show the target area; and at another an officer who passed to his chief an interpretation showing that an attack had missed its mark found it later on his desk with scrawled across it in red: 'I do not accept this report.' But such a reaction seems less unreasonable if it is regarded in the light of a long-standing attitude towards photography within Bomber Command. Photographs were considered as a useful adjunct to bombing, but not a vital necessity. The camera was regarded somewhat as a motorist regards his mileage gauge. It's nice to know how far you've been, and sometimes very useful too. But you certainly do not expect your mileage gauge to turn round and accuse you of having lost your way almost every time you've been out. When the photographs began to do precisely this, it was very natural that many of those whose work it affected jumped to the comforting conclusion that something must have been wrong with the camera or the photographs or the man who wrote the report.

But within a matter of months, as the true situation was realized more and more at the Stations and Groups, everyone with responsibility in Bomber Command was profoundly troubled by its seriousness. Sir John Slessor has stated in his book *The Central Blue* that at 5 Group during the summer of 1941 it was his principal preoccupation to find ways of improving navigational and bombing accuracy; but he frankly admits that he knew nothing more than rumours of the experiments with navigational aids that were already beginning at the Telecommunications Research Establishment.

There was one man, however, who could view the whole field of British scientific development, and whose opinions on such matters carried as much weight as those of the whole Air Force put together. Professor Lindemann, in his unique position at Churchill's elbow, had for some time been seriously worried about the accuracy of British bombing, and in the summer of 1941 Churchill asked him to make a thorough investigation. The Professor and his statisticians descended on Bomber Command, and rapidly gathered the facts they needed. It was a moment when the whole future of British bombing hung in the balance. The report which Lindemann submitted to Churchill summed up the evidence of the night photographs taken during the months of June and July 1941. By then Bomber Command had more night cameras, but there were still not nearly enough to go round, and they were usually allotted to the most efficient crews; so there was no doubt that things were actually quite a lot worse than could be proved by figures. But the figures were bad enough. They showed that only one aircraft in every four claiming to have attacked their objectives had got within five miles of its target. Churchill has recorded his views on the matter in *The Second World War*:

The air photographs showed how little damage was being done. It also appeared that the crews knew this, and were discouraged by the poor results of so much hazard. Unless we could improve on this there did not seem much use in continuing night bombing.

Professor Lindemann's report went on to the Chief of the Air Staff, Air Chief Marshal Sir Charles Portal, with a Minute from the Prime Minister:

This is a very serious paper and seems to require your most urgent attention. I await your proposals for action.

So it was at these topmost levels that the evidence of the photographs was finally faced, and at these levels that the necessary priority was given to developing the new navigational aids – 'Gee', 'Oboe', and 'HS' – which were to change the entire outlook for British night bombing.

•   •   •

Meanwhile the Spitfires from Oakington had been pressing on with their daylight reconnaissance. It was well that the Spitfire was so much faster than the Me 109; for the pilots who went out on the 'DA' sorties knew that the enemy fighters would always be on the alert for them. The Germans were fully aware that we would want to check the results of an attack without delay – if possible the next morning – and naturally they were waiting to revenge the hurt of the night before.

During the six months that Pat Ogilvie was commanding 3 PRU, he flew many operational sorties himself, and often the tiles of Coton Manor rattled as Pat's Spitfire swooped joyously over to announce his return; but he also made time to nip over frequently to Farnborough, where his sturdy figure and explosive laughter were as well known as at Bomber Command –

and also his practical jokes. The intricacies of the cameras were Pat's concern just as much as the long cold flights; for the foremost function of his unit was 'to obtain photographs of bombing targets at a scale suitable for the assessment of damage'; and the crucial word in this brief was the word 'scale'.

Pat's first introduction to aerial cameras had been at the RAF School of Photography at Farnborough some years earlier, when he learnt that even if you fly much higher, the scale of your photographs need not diminish if you fit a lens with a longer focus. And while at the school he visited the Photographic Division of the Royal Aircraft Establishment, and there met Harry Stringer. Since then they had kept closely in touch, and after Pat took command of 3 PRU he often turned to Stringer for advice and help.

'I was over at Bomber again,' Pat told Stringer on one of his visits to Farnborough, 'and it's the same old story. The Operations people say the damage is there all right, but that the interpreters can't see it because the scale is so small. There's nothing you can answer to that.'

'No; except "just you wait",' answered Stringer, as Pat surreptitiously slipped some gunpowder into the ashtray. 'When our 36-inch lens is ready they'll have to think again.'

The fact of the matter was that although, at this stage of the war, the scale of most of the photographs was inadequate for damage assessment, the bombs then being dropped were doing negligible damage. But that was not the point as far as Pat and his pilots were concerned. It was their job to try for photographs of the targets the bombers had been after, and this they did very effectively with the equipment that was then available.

Later on, in 1942, when the 36-inch lenses came into use, there was a great leap forward both in 'sharpness' and in scale. Then, on photographs taken from many miles up, one could occasionally see the tiny dark specks that represented the human beings so far below. They didn't really look like ants – the obvious simile – but more like grains of pepper, hardly noticeable individually, but springing to the eye when in the mass: for instance when a shift of workers was pouring out of the gates of an aircraft factory. I sometimes used to think that photographic interpretation was a nice clean job, as even after the heaviest attacks, and even with the largest scale, you never saw any blood. As new interpreters were taught, a vertical air photographis is not a picture but a precise mathematical document.

It was a fitting climax to Pat Ogilvie's time with 3 PRU that he himself should get the first reconnaissance photographs of Berlin; and as if it was not enough to secure this daylight cover, he went off in a Wellington equipped with cameras for night reconnaissance, and photographed the capital by flashlight. That first cover of Berlin was achieved in a manner typical of Pat, with an incongruous mixture of efficiency, skill, and the carefree irresponsibility of a schoolboy on a bicycle ride. The Berlin photographs were a great feather in the cap of Bomber Command, and within two weeks Pat was awarded the DSO. But after reaching these heights, the fortunes of 3 PRU began to decline.

At the Air Ministry new plans for reorganizing photographic intelligence were hatching out, and the question whether it was desirable for Bomber Command to have its own reconnaissance unit was raised once more. And at the same time Pat Ogilvie was chosen to take command of the first squadron of Stirlings. In May 1941 the life and soul of 3 PRU departed from it.

Bernard carried steadily on with the research that he and Pat had started together, and by this time he was delving deeper into the esoteric mysteries of night photographs. Week by week he was accumulating material for a report summarizing the principles of this specialized new branch of interpretation. In order to help the Station Intelligence Officers, he was going to explain all he had discovered about the various strange markings which find their way on to films exposed at night. To the untrained eye some of those photographs look like nothing more than a chaotic muddle of wavy white lines and streaks and splodges; rather like the efforts of a three-year-old let loose with a box of chalks. But Bernard has the sort of mind which enjoys making calculations depending on five or six variables, and he could translate the crazy-looking scrawls into precise facts. He used to explain to me that any lights which showed in the darkness below the camera while the shutter was open appear on the photographs as streaks, because the exposure was often as long as five seconds, and unless the aircraft were flying straight and level the streaks would naturally undulate according to its movement – in other words they were an exact record of all the manoeuvres it had made. They were also, of course, a record of the many different kinds of light that go with an air attack: the fires and the bomb flames; and also the tracer, the heavy flak, and the searchlights of the defences. But Bernard did not confine his analysis to individual photographs: he soon became interested in working out the relationship between photographs taken by several bombers on the same raid, allowing for the different headings and evasive actions of each, so as to calculate the progress of the fires on the ground.

He was deep in calculations of fire tracks and flak bursts, of bank and drift and timing, when in June 1941 he heard that 3 PRU was going to close down. For a time he stayed on at Oakington as a Station Intelligence Officer, but before long he was starting up a night photograph section at the Central Interpretation Unit.

Perhaps the experiment of an independent Bomber Command PRU had to be tried out. If it had never been actually tried, some people would always have claimed that it might have worked. But the principle 'contract to expand' was steadily proving itself and the time of contracting was almost over. When 3 PRU came to an end,* and its pilots and Spitfires moved to Benson, it was an important step towards the formation – two years later – of a photographic reconnaissance Wing, and later still of an RAF Group entirely devoted to the needs of photographic intelligence.

•   •   •

Early in 1941, not long after Peter Riddell had asked me to start an aircraft section, the Photographic Interpretation Unit moved from Wembley to a safer and more pleasant spot. Its new home was a large pseudo-Tudor mansion called Danesfield; a pretentious edifice of whitish-grey stone, with castellated towers and fancy brick chimneys, which looks out southwards from a magnificent site high above the Thames between Marlow and Henley.

When Danesfield became an Air Force Station it had to be given an official title, and it was named 'RAF Station Medmenham', after the little riverside village near by. From then on, for the rest of the war, the name 'Medmenham' – which in the eighteenth century had been linked with black magic because the first headquarters of the 'Hell Fire Club' was at Medmenham Abbey – was identified with photographic intelligence. Some people, at the time, thought it was rash of the Air Ministry to take on such a big house at Danesfield. The Commander-in-Chief of Coastal Command, in particular, felt it was much too large. But during the years that followed, RAF Station Medmenham grew a crop of mammoth-sized huts which almost dwarfed the country mansion itself.

---

* The title No. 3 PRU was used again later when a Photographic Reconnaissance Unit was started in India.

At this stage, in the summer of 1941, the control of photographic intelligence was entrusted to the Air Staff's new Chief of Intelligence, Air Vice-Marshal Charles Medhurst (who had himself flown photographic sorties in the First World War). He looked round for someone to organize the expansion at Medmenham on the lines he wanted. Wing Commander Peter Stewart, an officer of the Auxiliary Air Force, had just made a great success of organizing a new War Room at the Air Ministry, and Medhurst chose him to head a new Assistant Directorate of Photographic Intelligence, or ADI (Ph.), as it was usually called. Later Stewart came to Medmenham as commanding officer.

Stewart's first move was to 'militarize' the unit, which meant that for a start the Aircraft Operating Company's personnel who were still civilians had to get into uniform. In time it also meant that some of the leading spirits of the Wembley regime, such as Michael Spender and Peter Riddell, took their leave. The Central Interpretation Unit, as it had been renamed, was entering a period of somewhat severe growing pains. The 'kicking child', as Sidney Cotton had once called it, had reached the struggles of adolescence.

●　　●　　●

At Medmenham Douglas Kendall was in charge of the Second Phase section, which worked on day and night shifts in one of Danesfield's palatial halls. Outside the high west windows was a mass of mauve wisteria, and the sweet heavy scent drifted into Second Phase. I remember it well, as the desk which was the Aircraft Sections's first home – where I pondered all day over German fighters and bombers – was just near one of the windows.

Kendall was silent over his stereoscope, much intrigued by something he had just found. He was looking at some open fields near the German town of Soest, which lies just east of the Ruhr. After a bit he got up, thought for a minute, glanced round the room, and then went over to a desk where an interpreter called Geoffrey Dimbleby was bent low over some photographs.

'I expect you're frightfully busy, aren't you?' asked Kendall tentatively.

'Well, no, not if you want me to do something else.'

'Have a look at this and see if *you* know what it is' said Kendall, giving him a pair of photographs.

Dimbleby had a look, and saw the neat rectangular pattern of narrow German fields, with scattered over them the disfiguring splodges of bomb craters, dozens and dozens of them – perhaps about a hundred.

'One of the Ruhr raids gone wrong, isn't it?'

'Yes, I know,' said Kendall, 'but I mean *this*.' He pointed to some strange objects, the size of foundations for three large barns. They looked rather like three gigantic dominoes, laid close together.

'What on earth . . . ?'

'I'll tell you what I'm pretty sure it is,' said Kendall. 'A decoy. A fire site to draw off the bombers. I've been on the lookout for something like this; but this is the first one I've actually seen. Would you like to try and find out how it works?'

Dimbleby set to work to analyse the giant dominoes. The three rectangules had walls only five feet high – he could measure this from the shadows – and there were gaps in the walls, and no roofs of any kind. Then within the enclosures were bundles of stuff that looked like straw, set up at regular intervals. If the straw were set ablaze there would be a mass of flame inside the rectangles, and seen from a bomber far above it would strongly suggest a group of burning buildings. The report on the Soest decoy was received with some disfavour at Bomber Command. Really! What would the interpreters come up with next? It was all very well if the crews were sharp enough to recognize decoy fires and avoid them, but the interpreters seemed to spend their whole time in cutting away the ground from under your feet. They'd probably soon be proving that all the attacks had been aimed at decoys.

Dimbleby's report on Soest was, in fact, the first of many, and soon he was running a specialist Decoy Section. There was plenty to keep him busy, for the German decoy system was already widespread, and it became more and more elaborate as time went on.

Peter Stewart was well aware that 'the photographs', of both the day and night varieties, were a thorn in the side of Bomber Command. One day as he drove from London to High Wycombe he racked his brains to think how to make things less difficult. After lunch in the Mess he sat for a while in the ante-room, again searching for a way to make for better understanding. He glanced idly round the room, and then suddenly caught his breath. He had just noticed that Air Vice-Marshal Saundby was deep in the *Illustrated London News* and that all round the room the picture magazines and the illustrated papers were being looked at, while most of the other papers were lying untouched. What photographic intelligence needed was promotion. The raw material was flowing in every day; all that was wanted was the right presentation to make it really interesting.

As soon as he got back to the Air Ministry Stewart started planning a mock-up, and the moment it was ready he hurried to Medhurst.

'Can we really do this?' asked Medhurst, enchanted.

'Yes, sir,' Steward nodded emphatically, 'we can. And we must have a different cover each week; not like those dreary intelligence summaries that always look the same.'

The mock-up went on to the Chief of the Air Staff, and came back with just two words of comment: 'Excellent. Proceed.' Stewart proceeded at once, and his efforts brought into being an official picture magazine called

Evidence in Camera, which many pilots maintain was the only official publication they ever looked at.

There is no doubt that *Evidence in Camera* helped things a bit at Bomber Command, but only on the surface. In the later years of the war it was a different story. Then Sir Arthur Harris had his own special album of enlargements and his own special stereoscope viewers. But in the early years there was no real reconciliation between Bomber Command, with its hopes and fears and its agonizing difficulties, and the merciless revelations of the photographs.

FIVE

THE SEA WAR

From the very first day of the war, when Sidney Cotton's distant obliques of Wilhelmshaven proved so valuable, the importance and potentialities of photographic intelligence were realized at the Admiralty more clearly, perhaps, than anywhere else. All through 1940, 'Ned' Denning and the other officers of the Operational Intelligence Centre came to rely more and more on the interpretations from Wembley, and they also began to find that reports from other sources could be very effectively checked by means of photographic evidence.

At first the interpretation of ships was mainly a matter of measuring and identifying. But then early in 1941, as covers of the German shipyards gradually accumulated, there came a new development which immediately brought about quite a revolution in the methods of estimating U-boat production.

The interpretation of shiphards was the special province of a young man named David Brachi, one of the employees of the Aircraft Operating Company and a disciple of Michael Spender's. As soon as each new sortie was available, Brachi pounced on the cover of the shipyards; and he learnt, little by little, the methods and tempo of each individual yard. He allotted a code number to each new submarine as soon as its keel was laid down, and then watched and noted its progress on each successive cover. By the end of February 1941 the time had come to summarize his findings, and the report he produced set a precedent for the rest of the war:

his reports on shipbuilding became a regular institution. It also marked a new departure in interpretation, for its most startling news was a *forecast* of future U-boat production.

•   •   •

One day shortly after the move to Medmenham, late in the afternoon, most of the tables in the Second Phase room at Wembley were clear, as the day's sorties had not yet arrived. The night-shift interpreters were not due for another hour. But the desk where David Brachi was working was weighed down with stacks of box-files and book-shaped cardboard boxes full of photographs.

In a clearing among the photographs Brachi's head was bent so low that he might have been hoping to burrow the information out of the pictures with his nose. He set aside his stereoscope and reached for his measuring magnifier – a small precision instrument something like a jeweller's glass (it was actually intended for counting the threads of textiles to check the regularity of the weave, which gives an idea of its magnification and accuracy). He placed it on one of the prints, and under the crystal-clear lens, the metal scale calibrated in tenths of millimetres rested upon the image of something that looked like a slim grey splinter, with a darker grey knob jutting up half way along it. That 'splinter' was in fact a newly launched 500-ton submarine which was being fitted out and would soon be fighting in the waters of the Atlantic.

Brachi pencilled down a figure and took up his slide-rule; then handed the photograph and the magnifier to a young WAAF who was working at the other side of the big desk.

'See what you make her, Bunny,' he said.

Assistant Section Officer 'Bunny' Grierson, his indispensable assistant and partner, was responsible for checking every measurement and conversion, so in this way no interpretation was made without a double check.

'215 feet,' said 'Bunny' in a few moments.

'Yes,' said Brachi. 'So they're right up to time, and she ought to be ready for trials by mid-May.' He had been watching the progress of this particular submarine on the slips since the previous summer. By this time Brachi had watched many of the German shipyards from month to month and knew that the 500-ton U-boats were usually off the slips in eight months. Fitting out took another two or three. So as soon as a keel was laid down, he could add a finished submarine to the production estimate for eleven months ahead.

He sat back for a minute, took off his horn-rimmed glasses and gave them a rub with his handkerchief.

'It's a pity Spender's always away on First Phase now,' he said thoughtfully. 'I'd have liked to go over these new covers with him before I work out the final production estimate. We must do that tomorrow.' He crouched down again over his photographs, and was immediately lost in contemplation of the Germania slips at Kiel.

Next day he sought out Peter Riddell. 'I think you ought to see our figures for U-boat production,' he said with a secretive little smile. 'The totals are just ready.' Riddell went over the figures with him, and then sprang to his feet exclaiming, 'I must get Denning at once.'

On the following afternoon, Captain John Godwin, RM, who was responsible for the study of German ship-building at the Admiralty, was sent down to 'Paduoc House'.

'I'd like you to tell me how you have made your deductions,' he said to Brachi. 'How can you possibly tell from photographs what launchings to expect six months ahead?'

Brachi's dark little eyes twinkled. 'I'll show you, sir. I've got some stereo pairs ready. Here first of all at the Blohm and Voss yard is a keel that's just been laid down for a 500-tonner.'

Godwin had never used a stereoscope before, and at first all he could see was a confusing double image.

Brachi checked the position of the prints. 'Now try again, sir.' He pointed to the U-boat keel with a pencil. 'Oh yes, I've got it now,' said Godwin. 'Yes, I can see the keel. Let's have some more.'

Brachi put another pair of photographs in position. 'This is the same keel when the sections of the midships portion of the hull were just going to be put into position. There's the crane. And now here's another yard, Deschimag at Bremen,' he went on, 'and *these* photographs were taken a month after a new keel was laid down. The midships part of the hull has been finished, and the camouflage "cradle" is being put up over it.'

'I see,' said Godwin. 'Yes, I do see.'

'Now here, sir,' Brachi continued, 'is a later cover of the same submarine, and the "cradle" has been extended fore and aft. That's because the hull has been extended to its full length, so they've had to lengthen the "cradle" to screen it. The Germans are so methodical about their camouflage that once you get to know their methods you can tell quite a lot from the camouflage itself.' Brachi produced yet another pair of photographs and set them in place. 'And now this is a cover taken six months after the laying of the keel, and you see what's happening.'

'They've taken away some of the camouflage,' said Godwin.

'Yes, they've had to remove some of the "cradle" so as to finish work on the conning tower,' Brachi explained. 'And the day before yesterday *these* photographs came in. As you see the whole "cradle" has been removed, so that means she'll be launched any moment now.'

By the end of the afternoon Godwin was more than convinced: he was carried away. But he hardly dared to think what the photographic evidence was going to mean in terms of Allied shipping losses. As he got up to go he took a last look at Brachi's calculations.

'There's no doubt then. If we allow for the yards that haven't been covered, we can definitely expect a doubled production of U-boats four months from now. Ten this month, and at least twenty in July. My God!'

Back at the Admiralty, Godwin prepared an urgent new appreciation of the U-boat production programme, based almost entirely on Brachi's figures. It was at once submitted to Admiral Godfrey, the Director of Naval Intelligence. Next day Sir Dudley Pound raised the matter at a meeting of the Chiefs of Staff, and from there the new production estimate went on to the Prime Minister. It was very shortly after this, on 6 March 1941, that the 'Battle of the Atlantic' directive was written.

• • •

The lifelines of Britain were threatened not only by the U-boats but by the capital ships of the German Fleet: the *Hipper*-class cruisers, the pocket-battleships, the sister battle-cruisers *Scharnhorst* and *Gneisenau*, and the newly completed battleship *Bismarck*. The last named of these, and, at a later date, the *Tirpitz*, were the most powerful warships in the world. If any of these ships got loose in the Atlantic, they could massacre the big Allied convoys; and from the end of 1940 onwards it was a major responsibility of PRU to cooperate with Naval Intelligence in watching them.

This was the main reason why Flights had been sent to St Eval and Wick. From St Eval the Spitfires could cover Brest and the Biscay ports; and from the remote airfield on the bare cliffs of Caithness they could range up and down the Norwegian coast ready to spot any German ships that were creeping towards the open seas.

It was after the Flights had been operating for a few months from these two bases that Michael Spender started agitating for First Phase interpreters to be sent to join them. Immediate news ought to be reported on the spot. So a few interpreters set off from Wembley, and one of them was David Linton, who arrived at St Eval on New Year's Day 1941, after only two months as an interpreter.

That winter was an exceptionally cold one: Cornwall was deep in snow, and the sea spray froze in icicles on the cliffs. In Brittany the landscape was snow-covered too, and the photographs were consequently difficult to interpret as the light reflected by the snow blurred all the outlines and distorted the shapes. On his second day at St Eval, Linton joined another interpreter, more experienced than himself, in examining a new cover of Brest. The latter was much preoccupied with searching for U-Boats, and he delegated to Linton the job of measuring up the big stuff. Soon Linton told him that he had found 'something very big' in one of the dry docks. His find was more than 650 feet long, and his first thought was: 'I must find out what this boat is. If she's that size, her name must be in the book.' But he couldn't resist showing the 'boat' to his colleague at once. The shape of the vessel was hard to distinguish because of patches of snow on the deck and superstructure, and Linton was advised to report it cautiously as 'probably a merchant vessel'. But when the photographs reached Wembley, Michael Spender nearly jumped out of his skin, and dashed to the telephone to tell Denning that the *Admiral Hipper* had arrived at Brest.

Towards the end of January 1941, Spender came down to St Eval and told them that the Admiralty was worried about Norway. The Station Intelligence Officers at Wick had been doing their best at immediate reporting, but trained interpreters were badly needed. Linton was chosen to start up the new First Phase section and soon he was on his way to the North of Scotland.

At Wick David Linton built up a most efficient section, together with Assistant Section Officer Eve Holiday, the WAAF who had known all the answers on shipping in the oral exam at Wembley. Linton's pre-war experience as a geographer had given him a fund of knowledge about Scandinavia and also about meteorology and he could brief the pilots with real authority; while Eve, in her cheerful easygoing way, took a special interest in caring for their needs, and always had a hot cup of tea ready when a pilot returned cold and exhausted after hours of solitary flying.

It was from Wick, on 21 May 1941, that one of the most famous of all the early photographic sorties took place; the flight from which Pilot Officer Michael Suckling came back with the electrifying news that the *Bismarck* was on her way out to the Atlantic for the first time.

On that Wednesday morning an urgent phone call came to say that the Admiralty had news of 'German ships' steaming northwards in the Kattegat the day before. So 'the ships' (no hints were dropped as to what ships they might be) must be somewhere off the Norwegian coast, and within PRU range. PRU must find them.

Two Spitfires could be made ready; and the two pilots who were ready to fly them were Flying Officer Greenhill, an experienced DFC, and Michael Suckling, also an experienced pilot, but with such youthful looks – fair hair and blue eyes, invisible eyebrows and a pink and white face – that inevitably he was nicknamed 'Babe'.

Linton and Greenhill discussed the probabilities and agreed on a plan. Greenhill was to cover the coastline towards Oslo, because it seemed most likely that the ships might be there. Suckling, who was junior to Greenhill, was given the less responsible job of photographing the Bergen area.

As soon as the aircraft were brought to readiness, Suckling took off, at five minutes past eleven, and Greenhill followed just half an hour later. Both pilots refuelled at Sumburgh, which gave them an extra half-hour's range, and then set course for Norway.

Linton and Eve Holiday lunched as usual in the Officers' Mess, and then Eve went back to the interpretation section – the main downstairs room in a house that had been given over to PRU – this strange lodger unit that was a law to itself. Neither of the pilots was due back till late afternoon, so Linton went to write some letters in the ante-room at the Mess.

●　　●　　●

Michael Suckling in his Spitfire was flying high above the Norwegian coast towards Bergen from Sogne Fiord, where he had made landfall. Every minute or two he tipped over to port so as to cast a long look over the unending dark pattern of rocks and islands and inlets – or rather over the grey-blue water between them. Linton had marked on his map the most likely anchorages, but it was quite hard to pick them out.

He reached Herdla, the German fighter base, which was one of his secondary targets, and turned on his cameras briefly. Then on southwards, and as he was approaching Bergen from the west he suddenly caught sight of *them*. He threw the Spitfire into an almost vertical bank till he could see clearly, far far below – like tiny toy ships in a tiny model of a Norwegian fiord – not just one ship, but two, three, four, five, six! A big one – it must be a cruiser – and a destroyer, and four stubby merchant ships. He frantically skidded back straight and level and flicked on his cameras.

Good! That was that. Next he had to photograph Bergen itself, and then home. He made his run over the town, and was turning westwards when he was surprised to see yet more ships, anchored in the fiord five miles south of Bergen. It looked like another cruiser and four more merchantmen. Suckling banked right over as he reached them to make sure of his position, and then pulled the Spitfire back to take his photographs. Then he set course for home.

He had found the ships and photographed them, as well as his other targets, but that, of course, was only part of his tasks; it was not complete until he was safely home with his pictures. And for a solitary pilot in a single-engined plane, whose compass was his one and only navigational aid, it was not all that easy getting home to Wick from Norway. If you met unexpected upper winds and your navigation went wrong over the grey stretches of the North Sea, or when you were high over solid cloud – if you missed the Shetlands – you might easily go on and on over wide open sea until your fuel gave out and you went down into the Atlantic. Only a few weeks before, one PRU pilot had erred too far in the opposite direction, and after attempting a sortie to Trondheim had landed off the Northumberland coast, on Lindisfarne! So you had to keep your wits about you.

Just after 2.30 Eve Holiday was surprised to hear a Spitfire circling overhead, and she bustled out to the little Standard van which she and Linton used for getting about the airfield, and speeded over to the dispersal point. Suckling was back early because his search had met with such early success, and as he climbed out of the cockpit he broke the great news: 'I've seen them! Two of them!'

The waiting airmen had already taken the magazines out of the cameras and were off to the photographic section.

'Where's David?' asked Suckling. 'I must tell him about the ships.'

A few minutes later Linton heard the door at the other end of the long ante-room being opened softly, and he turned to see who it was. Suckling's beaming face was sticking round the big door, and Linton knew at once he had found the ships, even before the words were spoken: 'I've found them.'

'Come on in,' said Linton, crossing the room.

'I can't,' Suckling shook his head, 'I'm still in my flying-kit.' 'Babe' always took things very seriously, and would not transgress the rules of the Mess.

'Two of them,' he went on, 'and I think they're cruisers, or one might be a battleship.'

The first wartime course for RAF photographic officers, at RAF Farnborough in Hampshire from 19 November 1939 to mid-January 1940. Top row, left to right: Pilot Officers Esten, Archbald, Jones-Humphreys and Tomlinson; Warrant Officer Hayward (instructor). Bottom row, left to right: Pilot Officers Jonge and Blake; Flight Lieutenant Dunton (chief instructor); Pilot Officers May and Fyfe.
Roy Conyers Nesbit Collection

Spitfire pilots of the Special Survey Flight (the forerunner of No 212 Squadron) in France, 1940, before the Blitzkreig. In the centre: Flight Lieutenant R.H. 'Bob' Niven and Flight Lieutenant M.V. 'Shorty' Longbottom.
Jim Muncie Collection

Wing Commander F. Sidney Cotton, Commanding Officer of the Photographic Development Unit, showing photographs to Air Marshal Sir Arthur Barratt, Commander-in-Chief of the British Air Forces in France, in the spring of 1940. Cotton disliked being photographed, since some of his intelligence activities were clandestine.
Roy Conyers Nesbit Collection

Spitfire pilots of No 212 Squadron in June 1940 at the rear of a photographic trailer in the estate of the Duke of Orleans, awaiting the details of their photographic cover of the German advance. Left to right: Flying Officer C.T.V. 'Crackers' Craxton; Flight Lieutenant A.L. Taylor; Flight Lieutenant L.D. 'Tug' Wilson.
Jim Muncie Collection

Vehicles and equipment of No 212 Squadron in June 1940 at Fontenay-le-Comte airfield in France, ready to be blown up by the remainder of the ground crew before the men were evacuated to England. They included a petrol bowser, photographic trailers, trucks and a power unit.
Jim Muncie Collection

RAF officers in 1940, making a final check of a model of Kiel. This was the first made by the Model Section of the Photographic Interpretation Unit. They were made of rubber and could be rolled up for transportation.
Roy Conyers Nesbit Collection

Two of the earliest pilots of the Photographic Development Unit at Heston in Middlesex during early 1940. Left to right: Pilot Officer Spencer L. Ring and Pilot Officer S.G. 'Bill' Wise.
Roy Conyers Nesbit Collection

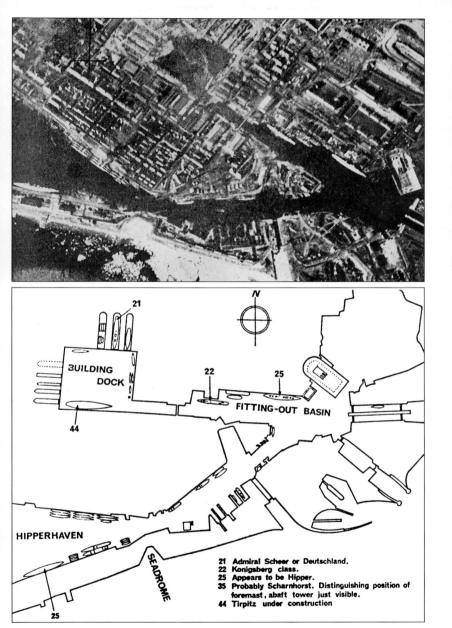

21 Admiral Scheer or Deutschland.
22 Konigsberg class.
25 Appears to be Hipper.
35 Probably Scharnhorst. Distinguishing position of
foremast, abaft tower just visible.
44 Tirpitz under construction

Interpretation of a photograph of Wilhelmshaven taken from 30,000 ft
on 2 March 1940.
Jim Muncie Collection

The country house of 'Danesfield' at Medmenham, between Marlow and Henley. It was taken over by the RAF after the Photographic Interpretation Unit at Wembley received a direct bomb hit on 2 October 1940. The organisation was renamed the Central Interpretation Unit on 7 January 1941 and then the Allied Central Interpretation Unit on 13 May 1944.
Roy Conyers Nesbit Collection

Wing Commander Douglas N. Kendall, who commanded the Photographic Interpretation section at Medmenham in Buckinghamshire. He was on the staff of the Aircraft Operating Company at Wembley before the war, which dealt in air photographs. On entering the RAF, he joined the small detachment of No 212 Squadron in France. He later devised the procedures for the RAF's photo-interpretation and trained its personnel.
Roy Conyers Nesbit Collection

Wing Commander Geoffrey W. Tuttle DFC, who took over command of the Photographic Reconnaissance Unit at Heston in June 1940 and was mainly responsible for its expansion until promoted and moved to other duties in November 1941.
Roy Conyers Nesbit Collection

The heavy cruiser *Admiral Hipper* in dry dock at Brest, photographed by Pilot Officer J.D. Chandler on 26 January 1941.
Roy Conyers Nesbit Collection

Flying Officer Michael F. Suckling, who photographed the *Bismarck* and *Prinz Eugen* in Norwegian Fjords on 21 May 1941.
Roy Conyers Nesbit Collection

Group Captain Fred Winterbotham, an intelligence officer who worked with Sidney Cotton before the war to secure photographs of German and Italian preparations. *Roy Conyers Nesbit Collection*

Group Captain Peter A. Riddell, who devised the highly successful photo-interpretation procedures followed by the RAF during the Second World War. *Roy Conyers Nesbit Collection*

The German Würzburg radar installation beside the sanitorium at Bruneval, near Cap d'Antifer on the north coast of France, photographed by Flight Lieutenant A.E. Hill on 5 December 1941. This led to the Commando raid in 1942.
Roy Conyers Nesbit Collection

Squadron Leader A.E. 'Tony' Hill, who took the photograph of the German radar installation at Bruneval.
Roy Conyers Nesbit Collection

The German battleship *Tirpitz* in Aasfjord near Trondheim, photographed on
28 March 1942 by Flight Lieutenant Alfred F.P. Fane.
Roy Conyers Nesbit Collection

The Italian naval base of Taranto photographed from 16,000 ft on
14 November 1940 by a Maryland of No 431 (General Reconnaissance)
Flight from Luqa in Malta.
Roy Conyers Nesbit Collection

The airfield of Focus near Trondheim photographed on 14 March 1941 by a Spitfire of No 1 Photographic Reconnaissance Unit based at Wick in Caithness. The interpreters were able to identify runway improvements and buildings under construction by the German occupying force. *Jim Muncie Collection*

Flight Officer Constance Babington Smith examining air photographs through a stereoscope, which gave the impression of depth and solidity to the viewer. *The late Constance Babington Smith*

The Control Section of the Photographic Department, Allied Central Intelligence Unit at RAF Medmenham. It was staffed jointly by British and Americans.
Roy Conyers Nesbit Collection

The RAF photography and film negative library at Medmenham.
Roy Conyers Nesbit Collection

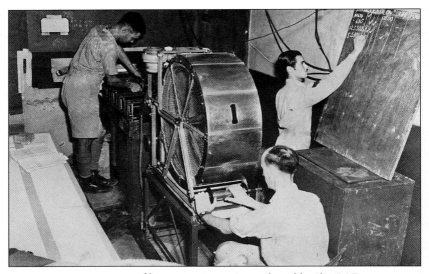

A continuous film processing unit employed by the RAF.
Roy Conyers Nesbit Collection

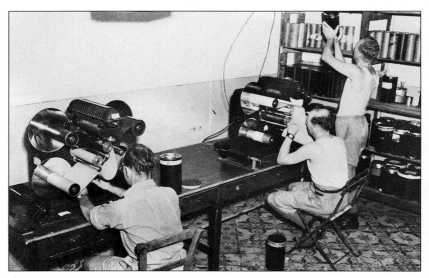

Film duplicating equipment employed by the RAF.
Roy Conyers Nesbit Collection

Above: The port of Rhodes occupied by the Germans, photographed on 4 December 1942 by No 2 Photographic Reconnaissance Unit based at LG219 near Heliopolis in Egypt.
Roy Conyers Nesbit Collection

Right: An undated photograph of an attack by the US Eighth Air Force against the port of La Pallice, from where U-boats were operating in the Atlantic.
Roy Conyers Nesbit Collection

General-purpose bombs of 1,000 lb falling on the naval base at Wilhelmshaven during an attack on 27 January 1943 by B-17 Flying Fortresses of the US Eighth Air Force, its first attack on Germany. Only one aircraft was lost from the 55 despatched, but 32 others were damaged.
Roy Conyers Nesbit Collection

Bombs exploding on the Chemische Werke at Hüls in Germany during an attack by B-17 Fortresses and B-24 Liberators on 22 June 1943.
Roy Conyers Nesbit Collection

A Spitfire PR XI which originally operated from Mount Farm in Oxfordshire, one of the bases of the US Eighth Air force. It is preserved in its blue livery at the Wright Patterson Air Force base in Ohio.
Roy Conyers Nesbit Collection

Part of the airfield at Sabratha (Sabrata in Roman times), on the coast about fifty miles west of Tripoli. Some airfield buildings can be seen at the top of the photograph, above the Roman amphitheatre. This was a Luftwaffe base until the Germans were driven out, shortly before this photograph was taken on 2 February 1943. No 60 (SAAF) Squadron was later based there, employing its Mosquito PR IVs, VIs and IXs on photo-reconnaissance of Sicily prior to the Anglo-American invasion of the island on 9/10 July 1943.
Roy Conyers Nesbit Collection

Colonel Karl 'Pop' Polifka, a renowned photo-reconnaissance pilot of the USAAF.
Roy Conyers Nesbit Collection

General Sir Harold Alexander (Deputy Allied C-in-C in the North African theatre of war) pointing to a map of Italy with a group of Allied reconnaissance officers. This was at the headquarters of the North African Photographic Reconnaissance Wing at La Marsa in Tunisia, prior to the invasion of Italy.
Jack Eggleston Collection

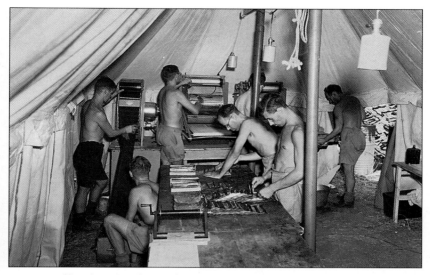

A film-drying and print-finishing tent at Lentini in Sicily in 1943.
Jack Eggleston Collection

Three photo-interpreters of the WAAF: Ann McKnight-Kauffer (above); Sarah Oliver, daughter of Winston Churchill (below, left) and Eve Holiday (below, right).
The late Constance Babington Smith

A high-level vertical of the battleship Tirpitz in Kaa fjord, off Alten fjord, taken in the autumn of 1943 by a photo-reconnaissance Spitfire of No 543 Squadron based at Vaenga in North Russia. The photograph was gridded for use by the photo-interpreters.
Roy Conyers Nesbit Collection

The US Eighth Air Force made its first attack against Norwegian targets on 24 July 1943. Among those despatched were 180 B-17 Flying Fortresses to the Farbenindustrie Combine's aluminium factory at Heroya, 65 miles south-east of Oslo. This photograph shows bombs falling towards a target area outlined with a broken white line. One Fortress was lost in this operation.
Roy Conyers Nesbit Collection

The town of Cassino in Italy after destruction by Allied bombing on 15 March 1944.
Jack Eggleston Collection

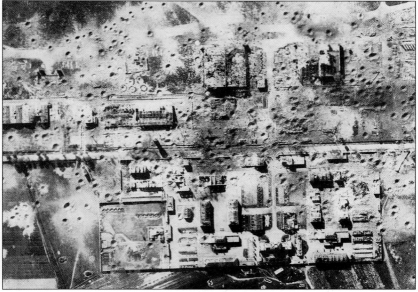

The destruction of the airfield at Tours after a series of very accurate attacks. The US Eighth Air Force despatched forty-five P-38 Lightnings on 28 April 1944, and 1,000 lb bombs were dropped for the loss of one aircraft. The next took place two days later, when forty-four Lightnings attacked without loss. RAF Bomber Command despatched fifty-three Lancasters and eight Mosquitos on the night of 7/8 May 1944, obliterating most of the remaining buildings for the loss of two aircraft.
Roy Conyers Nesbit Collection

Low-level oblique of the main railway station at Florence in Tuscany. This major cultural and artistic centre did not suffer the serious damage of other cities during the war.
Roy Conyers Nesbit Collection

The famous bridges at Nijmegen in the Netherlands, connecting the country with Germany over the river Waal (Rhine). One of the main objectives of the great Allied airborne operation of 17 September 1944 at Arnham was to capture these bridges intact. The railway bridge is at the top of the photograph and the road bridge at the bottom.
Roy Conyers Nesbit Collection

Anti-invasion 'Hedgehog' obstacles inland from the beach near Dunkirk, photographed by a low-flying aircraft of the US Ninth Air Force.
Roy Conyers Nesbit Collection

Bomber Command despatched seventy-two aircraft on 27 July 1944 to attack flying bomb sites in north-east France, as shown in this photograph of a Lancaster. The targets were cloud-covered and some of the aircraft bombed using G-H radar instead of visual bombsights. No aircraft were lost.
Roy Conyers Nesbit Collection

The lock gates of the Kembs dam, across the Rhine near Mulhouse, were the target for thirteen Lancasters of No 617 Squadron in daylight on 7 October 1944, to prevent the Germans from flooding the valley in the path of advancing American and French troops. US Mustangs supressed flak while the attack took place, as shown in this explosion of a 12,000 lb bomb. The lock gates were put out of action but two Lancasters were shot down.
Roy Conyers Nesbit Collection

Lieutenant-General Lewis H. Brereton of the USAAF making the award of the American Bronze Star to Squadron Leader R. Idris Jones of the RAF, who was seconded to his Allied Airborne Army. Jones was a senior interpretation officer who was condemned to death *in absentia* by the Germans after they found his signature on some secret documents captured during the fall of France, but of course they could never carry out the sentence.
Roy Conyers Nesbit Collection

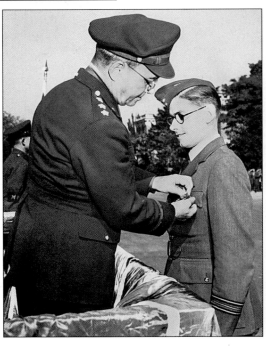

An enormous explosion took place in the Vaagen quay of Bergen towards the end of April 1944. RAF photo-interpreters were able to judge the extent of the destruction along a front of 150 yards of the quay (A). These were the tug (B) and the two small boats (C) thrown on the quay, and the 180 ft passenger packet ship capsized. Parts of the old Bergenhus Castle (E) which were being used by the Germans for administration (1), the Haakon's Hall Museum (2) housing some fine old tapestries, and the Rosenkranz Tower (3), had all suffered severely. Some of the buildings damaged south-west of the harbour were the Customs Office (F), a school (G) and the Nykirken (H). The inset showed the quay before the explosion.

Roy Conyers Nesbit Collection

A Frenchman waving to an Allied photo-reconnaissance aircraft over enemy-occupied territory on 20 July 1944.
Roy Conyers Nesbit Collection

A Tempest V in hot pursuit of a V-1 flying bomb, which can be discerned near the top of this photograph. RAF fighters were allocated an area over the English country-side, between the anti-aircraft batteries along the south-east coast and the balloon defences on approaches to London. Tempests were the fastest of these fighters and were credited with destroying 638 flying bombs.
Roy Conyers Nesbit Collection

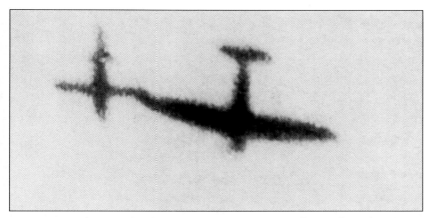

A very rare photograph of a Spitfire tipping the wing of a V-1 flying bomb to cause it to crash and explode in open country. The Spitfire did not have the speed to catch these bombs in level flight and must have caught it after a dive.
Roy Conyers Nesbit Collection

An oblique and a vertical of the famous raid on Amiens Prison by forty-four Mosquitos of the RAF's Second Tactical Air Force on 19 February 1945. The purpose was to bomb the German quarters and breach the outer wall, to enable French prisoners to escape.
Roy Conyers Nesbit Collection

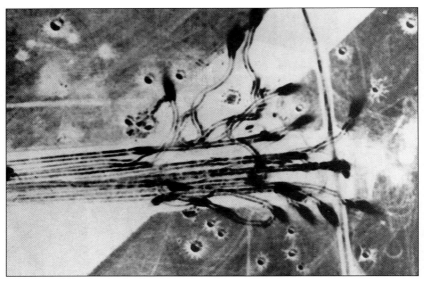

A vertical taken by an RAF photo-reconnaissance aircraft of the German airfield at Rheine, east of Osnabruck, a base for Messerschmitt Me262 jets which began to enter service in May 1944. Note the scorch marks on the ground, caused by the engines when starting up, as well as the bomb craters.
Roy Conyers Nesbit Collection

A vertical taken by an RAF photo-reconnaissance aircraft on 5 March 1945 showing a long line of German transport east of Swindemünde on the Baltic, retreating from the Russian onslaught at Dievenow.
Roy Conyers Nesbit Collection

Smoke rising from the factory area in south-west Berlin after raids by the US Eighth Air Force on 6 and 8 March 1944. In the former, 504 B-17 Flying Fortresses and 266 B-24 Liberators were despatched, escorted by 801 fighters; losses were 53 Fortresses, 16 Liberators and 11 fighters. In the latter, 404 Fortresses and 209 Liberators were despatched, escorted by 891 fighters; losses were 28 Fortresses, 9 Liberators and 18 fighters. The attacking force claimed to have shot down as many as 320 enemy fighters in these two raids. *Roy Conyers Nesbit Collection*

The Ludendorff railway bridge over the Rhine at Remagen, nine miles south-south-west of Bad Godesburg, photographed by a low-flying RAF reconnaissance aircraft. This was the famous bridge over which Lieutenant Karl Timmerman led his men of Company A, US 27th Armoured Infantry Battalion, on 7 March 1945, despite all the efforts of the German defenders to repel them. The Americans made good use of this bridge for the next ten days, although the Germans tried in every possible way to destroy it. *Roy Conyers Nesbit Collection*

A low-level oblique of the ruined city of Bremen on the river Weser, taken in 1945 by a photo-reconnaissance aircraft of the US Eighth Air Force.
Eric V. Hawkinson Collection

Bielefeld railway viaduct after it collapsed from the earthquake effect of 'Grand Slam' bombs of 22,000 lb and 'Tallboy' bombs of 12,000 lb dropped by No 617 Squadron on 14 March 1945.
Eric V. Hawkinson Collection

Constance Babington Smith joined the WAAF in July 1940, and after six months as a teleprinter operator was commissioned as a photographic interpreter. She started the Aircraft Section of the Central Interpretation Unit alone in April 1941, and was in charge of it throughout its expansion until 1945. She prepared training and reference material and lectured regularly to interpreters and at the RAF Staff College, the Empire Central Flying School etc. She was Mentioned in Dispatches in January 1942, and was awarded the MBE in 1945.

After VE-Day Flight Officer Babington Smith was lent to US Army Air Force Intelligence to continue interpretation work in the Pacific theatre. She received the Legion of Merit in December 1945, the first time the US Honour has been awarded to a British woman. Her citation says: 'Recognised as the outstanding Allied authority on the interpretation of photographs of aircraft, she provided the Eighth Air force with extremely vital intelligence for the strategic bombing and destruction of the German aircraft industry and contributed materially to the success of the USAF's strategic mission to Europe'.
Roy Conyers Nesbit Collection

A photograph was taken on 18 December 1941 when forty-seven aircraft of Bomber Command made a daylight attack on Brest. From this enlargement, photo-interpreters were able to identify the battleships *Scharnhorst* (1) and the *Gneisenau* (2) in their respective dry docks. Their previous white camouflage was partially missing, perhaps as a result of bombing. At (3) a dry dock under construction was picked out. Unusual camouflage was being constructed at (4) over burnt-out oil tanks, perhaps since these formed a conspicuous landmark.
Roy Conyers Nesbit Collection

Part of the Museum in the Joint School of Photography at RAF Cosford in 1990.
RAF Cosford

It was indeed a battleship. *The* battleship. And the chase *that followed, the epic chase that ended when the Bismarck* went to the bottom six days later, is among the best known and most exciting stories of the war.

Suckling's flight brought fame and glory to PRU, and his name will live because of it. But two months later to the day, the serious baby-faced young man took off on another photographic sortie, this time from St Eval to get pictures of La Rochelle, and he did not return. The histories tell of the flight over the Norwegian fiord on 21 May, and of the great events that followed it; but they do not tell of the Nottinghamshire home which on 21 July received the dreaded telegram, and mourned the son who had so briefly been a hero.

Suckling's visual report was sent out immediately, but as soon as Linton could get at the photographs he followed it up with a teleprinter signal, definitely identifying the *Bismarck* and the *Prinz Eugen*. He also added the important piece of news that when the photographs were taken the warships were not protected from torpedo attack by booms, which strongly suggested that they were about to move.

That very day Captain Clayton, who was in charge of the Admiralty's Operational Intelligence Centre, was visiting David Brachi's section at Medmenham for the first time. He was already, of course, very familiar with Brachi's reports, but he had never before actually seen for himself how interpretation was done. He spent the whole afternoon with Brachi, looking and listening with growing fascination. He was particularly interested in the way he was attempting to read the enemy's mind: interpreting motive by piecing together both positive and negative evidence after the manner of an archaeologist.

'We must keep in touch,' he said as he left.

Next morning at eleven o'clock Brachi's telephone rang. 'Clayton here.'

'Yes, sir.'

'You know the photographs I'm interested in?'

'Yes, sir.'

'I want you to look at them at once, and see if you can tell me what we want to know. Is she going raiding in the Atlantic? Or is it a sea-borne raid? Or are they just escorting a convoy of merchant vessels up the Norwegian coast?'

'How long can you give me, sir?'

'I've got to know before 12.30.'

Brachi tore down to Second Phase and advanced upon the Duty Interpretation Officer, his head slightly down as though to charge, and a dark worried frown on his face. Fortunately he was able to borrow the precious Bergen photographs and retreat unmolested.

At 12.30 he was on the telephone to Clayton. 'She must be going raiding, sir.'

'Why? What's the evidence?'

'I've worked it out by a process of elimination, sir,' said Brachi. 'They can't be going on a sea-borne raid, because none of the ships with them are troopships or assault vessels. But the fact that there's a tanker in the fiord suggests refuelling for a long trip. When I've seen other naval units preparing for trips up the Norwegian coast they've never been fuelled by special tanker. This is something out of the ordinary all right.'

'Good enough,' said Clayton with warm appreciation. 'We'd strongly suspected she was off on a raiding sortie, and this evidence of yours confirms it.'

●　　●　　●

How surprised the Celtic holy man named Eval would have been to know the circumstances in which his name was to become a household word in photographic intelligence a thousand years after his death. In 1941, at the busy RAF airfield which had once been Saint Eval's home ground, the reconnaissance of Brest was of supreme importance. It was 'Brest or bust' as the PRU pilots used to say.

The *Admiral Hipper*'s stay at the beginning of the year was brief, but in March the *Scharnhorst* and *Gneisenau* arrived after a foray in the Atlantic, and for almost a whole year, until their escape up the Channel, they were the most often photographed, and often bombed, target in Nazi Europe. Also the most ferociously defended: seven PRU pilots lost their lives as the price for the unceasing watch from St Eval.

At the end of May 1941, after the *Bismarck* went down, a whole week passed and the *Eugen* had still not been located. Where would she turn up? Flying Officer Gordon Hughes obtained the crucial answer. On 4 June he brought back pictures of the *Prinz Eugen* at Brest.

Gordon Hughes was fast becoming well known in PRU for his superb efficiency as a pilot, and also for his whimsical ways and original ideas, and for his great interest in his photographs. At St Eval he was always in and out of the Interpretation Section, hungry for the facts the interpreters had found, and gazing at the prints again and again. In the early days of the war, when there was so much uncertainty about the claims made in all honesty by bomber and fighter pilots, the pilots of PRU had the consolation of bringing back self-evident proof of what they had done.

Ann McKnight-Kauffer was one of the two interpreters at St Eval at this time, and one day when Gordon Hughes came in to look at his latest Brest pictures, she had just finished work on them.

'They're starting on some new flak positions here,' said Ann. Gordon looked at the prints that Ann had marked in Chinagraph pencil. 'And more fighters at Lanveoc Poulmic,' she went on, and then added impulsively, 'Do you ever wish you had guns yourself, Gordon?'

Gordon Hughes straightened himself up and looked at Ann with great earnestness.

'Oh *no*! *Never*! Don't you understand? That's the whole thing about PRU It's the only sort of front line job in this war where you aren't asked to kill. You have weapons of a different sort, which aren't guns – they're your planning and your flying and your . . . perseverance. I mean, the will to keep on when things go wrong and you're frozen to death. And don't you see, it's much more effective too. If someone who wants to pinch your flowers breaks down your gate, smashes the fence, and tramples down half your garden, you certainly don't let him get away with it. But if someone slips into your garden before you know it, picks some flowers and slips away again quietly and quickly, you may feel annoyed, but you probably let him go.'

All through the autumn and winter of 1941 the vigil over Brest was maintained, and during the time the battle-cruisers were there they were the objective of more than seven hundred photographic sorties. But on 12 February 1942, when the news came that they were well up the Channel before anyone in Britain knew they were on the move, it was a shock to everyone in photographic intelligence, as it was to the whole country. Not, however, because the break-out was unexpected.

During the last days of January many new arrivals were photographed at Brest: destroyers, torpedo-boats, mine-sweepers; and the fighter bases along the Channel coast began to bristle with Me 109s. Sortie after sortie showed that both the battle-cruisers and also the *Prinz Eugen* were nearly ready to move.

The Admiralty was already well aware what was in the wind. Their other intelligence sources had alerted them, and the photographs provided confirmation. At the Operational Intelligence Centre, 'Ned' Denning prepared an appreciation, making a confident forecast that there would soon be an attempt to get the ships back to Germany by way of the Channel.

Then on Sunday, 8 February, two pilots from St Eval took photographs of Brest which showed that preparations were extremely advanced. The *Scharnhorst* was 'emitting much smoke', and the *Gneisenau* was at moorings off Lanveoc. Two more destroyers had arrived and the mine-sweepers had gone off.

At the headquarters of Coastal Command, the Commander-in-Chief conferred with his intelligence staff. By this time Bowhill had been succeeded by Air Chief Marshal Sir Philip Joubert, to whom photographic intelligence was no newfangled idea, as he had been closely concerned with it in the First World War. The evidence of the photographs of Brest, along with the Admiralty appreciation, led him to send out an urgent warning, on 9 February, to his own Groups and also to the other Commands.

On the following day the weather was shocking, and not a single photograph of Brest could be secured. But on the Wednesday – 11 February – two Spitfires were successful. At four o'clock that afternoon both battle-cruisers were still there. But before midnight they were on their way towards the Channel.

Next morning when Douglas Kendall came into the long Second Phase room at Medmenham and said 'They've got away,' at first no one believed him.

'Whatever will they do with themselves at St Eval now,' exclaimed one of the interpreters, 'without Salmon and Gluckstein!'

It was as though a tooth which had long been aching had at last been drawn. The ache had gone, but instead there was a great yawning void.

• • •

Ever since the beginning of war, the photographic pilots had been flying the much-loved Spitfire, in successive versions with steadily increasing range; but there were still many important areas that were out of reach: East Prussia, south-east Germany, Czechoslovakia. So it had been a great day when Geoffrey de Havilland himself flew the RAF's first Mosquito over to Benson – in July 1941. The shapely twin-engined aeroplane had the range of a bomber and the performance of a fighter, and exciting new horizons began to open up.

It was decided that the first Flight of Mosquitos should operate from Wick, and Alistair Taylor was chosen to lead it. Taylor would have been an outstanding figure in whatever he chose to do – but in photographic reconnaissance he attained exceptional heights. He was in fact the first pilot in the whole war to be awarded two bars to his DFC. 'You could hardly see the ribbon for stars,' as one of his pilots said with awe.

But the combination of amazing skill and singlemindedness which earned him his decorations was only a beginning. The tall lean young man with a high forehead and remarkable piercing eyes had the arrogance of youth and few familiar friends, but he had vision and certainty and a quality which was something more than 'drive', for what Alistair Taylor wanted to do – what he thought was needed for PRU – he did without the seeming effort that quite often goes into 'drive'. This was largely because of the effect he had on the people round him. Apart from a few who reacted violently away from 'God' Taylor, and looked upon him as inhuman, those who came within his aura worshipped him and gladly slaved to meet his demands.

In October 1941 Taylor and the Mosquitos arrived at Wick and the Flight began to try its wings. Each aircraft was named after a different variety of strong drink: Whisky, Benedictine, Vodka. Later there were also Drambuie, Cointreau, and Crême de Menthe. At first some of the pilots found it very strange to have a navigator with them telling them where to go, but they soon got used to it, and also found out what tremendous advantages there are in having a crew of two. The pilots who became really familiar with the Mosquito got to love it whole-heartedly.

Before the Flight had been long at Wick, however, it became clear that a more convenient base would have to be found. There was an unduly long time-lag in sending the photographs to Medmenham, and in bad weather it might take four or five days to get Mosquito spare parts from the south. Now that aircraft with longer range were being used, it was not so necessary to operate from the extreme north of Scotland. By December the unit had moved to Leuchars, near the Firth of Forth.

It was bad, wintry weather, but the flying was started up again at once, and one of the first sorties was on 4 December when Taylor and his navigator, Sergeant Horsfall, set off in Mosquito W-4055 – alias Benedictine – for routine cover of Trondheim and Bergen.

When Benedictine was overdue, Eve Holiday and David Linton were not at first concerned, for Taylor was often overdue, and he always came back later. But this time he did not come back later. He and Horsfall, and the Mosquito called Benedictine, never came back.

The story of Taylor's last flight was gradually pieced together afterwards. It seems that the day he was lost was probably the first day the Germans used their new high-level anti-aircraft guns in Norway. And in time a story filtered through from Norway telling that one day early in December, a twin-engined aircraft of an unidentified new type was hit, and the pilot – if he had wished – could easily have crash-landed it safely. That would, of course, have meant delivering the aircraft to the Luftwaffe. Instead, the pilot used his height to turn out to sea, and was far out from the shore when he went down into the waves.

SIX

THE MEDITERRANEAN WATCH

While the PRU pilots were reaching out from Britain across the skies of northern Europe, photographic intelligence was beginning to come into its own further south. But to pick up the threads in the Mediterranean area means first of all taking a brief glance back to the beginning of the war, to the days when Fred Winterbotham and Sidney Cotton were cooperating to obtain 'unofficial' information for the Air Staff. When Cotton got into uniform and started the Heston Flight, in September 1939, his connexion with Winterbotham, as it had worked until then, was terminated. But they still kept closely in touch, and on occasion there were projects which concerned them both.

In March 1940 there was need for photographs of the Russian oilfields near the Caspian, which were suspected to be supplying the Germans. Winterbotham and Cotton were asked to help, and together they worked out a plan. From Habbaniya, the RAF base near Baghdad, it was 600 miles to Baku. An aircraft such as the Lockheed which they had used for their earliest photography could do it comfortably. To fly such a sortie, they would need an experienced pilot of the 'go anywhere, do anything' type, and Hugh Macphail, Cotton's personal assistant, fresh from flying DC-3s across the Andes, was a very suitable man for the job.

A week or so later Macphail left Heston for the Middle East in a civil Lockheed, G-AGAR, which had been specially equipped with hidden cameras. At Habbaniya the registration markings on the aircraft were painted out, and on 30 March the anonymous Lockheed took off for Baku. Macphail was accompanied by a co-pilot, Flying Officer Burton, and two airmen who were going to take additional photographs with a hand-held camera. They climbed north-eastwards across the mountains of Kurdistan, and then far ahead Macphail could see the Caspian. Jutting out into it was a solitary peninsula – the heart of Russia's oil supply. As he got nearer, he could see that the oil refineries stretched for miles along the shore, both southwards and northwards from the great industrial city of Baku. For an hour he flew unchallenged over the whole area, and at a considerable height made six runs over the endless conglomeration of oil tanks, derricks, and processing plants. When Macphail and his crew finally landed back at Habbaniya they had been flying for over nine hours.

Six days after this Macphail made a second sortie. On 5 April he photographed Batum, the Black Sea terminus of the pipeline from Baku. But this time he was interrupted in the middle of his work. On his second run he suddenly saw four black puffs of smoke, and then five more: bursts of anti-aircraft fire. He changed course hastily, and got away as rapidly as he could. But Batum had been photographed as well as Baku. Both of the surreptitious sorties had achieved their purpose.

At Heston ten days later Macphail delivered the precious films to Sidney Cotton, who took them to Wembley for interpretation. A detailed report accompanied by photographs was soon ready, and a copy was given to the French Deuxième Bureau.

Unfortunately, however, this report was not destroyed before the Germans took Paris, and among the interesting spoils of war that fell into their hands were some aerial photographs of Russia's greatest oil centre, along with a detailed English interpretation report. What splendid anti-British ammunition! It seems amazing, now, that only a year before Hitler invaded Russia the Germans and the Russians could rave together in 'righteous indignation' against the 'illicit tricks' of the British. No doubt a little later, when Hitler set his heart on capturing the oil of the Caucasus, the photographs of Baku found their place in the German target files. But in 1940, Hugh Macphail's sorties and the Wembley interpretation report caused a diplomatic flurry that left a deep mark, and gave photographic intelligence in the Middle East an aura of hushed-up notoriety that put it in a class with the best cloak-and-dagger spy stories.

•   •   •

In the turmoil of the first week of June 1940 – during the final days of Dunkirk – Sidney Cotton sent Hugh Macphail to the Middle East in G-AGAR for a second time. If Italy came into the war, new photographs of the Dodecanese might be very useful. When Macphail left Heston he reckoned he would be back in a couple of weeks.

A day or two after he reached Cairo, however, the Italians did declare war, and the new RAF Commander-in-Chief, Air Chief Marshal Sir Arthur Longmore, sent for Squadron Leader Macphail.

'What are you doing wandering about the Middle East?' he asked severely. Macphail explained that he had come out from England specially to photograph the Dodecanese, and was to return immediately afterwards. Longmore only had a handful of obsolescent aircraft for reconnaissance and he soon made it clear that G-AGAR would be a welcome addition to the strength of his Command, and that he would also be glad of Macphail's services. So the trip that was supposed to last a couple of weeks lasted for two and a half years, and G-AGAR was soon hard at work keeping an eye on the Italians in Libya.

Three months later, in September, two photographic interpreters arrived in Cairo from England, and after only a few weeks there was some extremely important interpretation to be done. Admiral Cunningham was laying his plans for attacking the Italian fleet at Taranto. For a start, therefore, he needed as much information as possible on the harbour defences, and he turned to the RAF for the essential preliminary reconnaissance.

Just before this an exciting event had occurred at Malta. A Flight of Marylands had arrived from Britain, and for the first time in the war the island's superb position as a base for photographic reconnaissance could be exploited. At this stage there was no question of sending out a unit of photographic Spitfires – PRU was only just getting into its stride at Heston – but the Marylands were more than equal to the intelligence needs of the day, and they also lent a hand in other directions. These twin-engined American-built aircraft, with a crew of three, were equipped for all contingencies, with guns and bomb racks as well as cameras, and the Maryland crews jumped at any chance of 'having a crack' that came their way.

When the Marylands started on their reconnaissance of Taranto the photographs were sent to Cairo for detailed interpretation, and there Flight Lieutenant R. Idris Jones set to work set to work on them. In his office at the RAF headquarters he laid out the overlapping prints on his desk, and before him the splendid semicircle of Taranto's outer harbour took shape. There, dotted in the curve of the harbour, lay the best part of the Italian fleet – battleships, cruisers, destroyers – the ships that would not come out to fight. He then got down to the detail, plotting the exact position of each ship, and of the elaborate booms. He could just see the faint tracery of the floats that held up the anti-torpedo nets – they showed up as lines of tiny grey blobs against the dark water of the harbour. Next he plotted two lines of white specks: the barrage balloons which protected the southern half of the harbour and part of the northern half.

His report went off to Cunningham's staff, along with copies of the photographs; but Jones was subsequently on the phone to the *Illustrious* several times, and he still recalls how dismayed he was to hear that his statement about the balloon barrage had been ignored. There had been no previous reports of Italian balloon barrages, he was told, and 'no one could see any balloons on the photographs'. In fact, the current plan for the attack meant that the aircraft would fly straight into both lines of balloons. Jones hurried to Group Captain Paynter, the Chief Intelligence Officer, who said they must both go at once to Longmore.

The Commander-in-Chief listened, and then looked carefully at the photographs on which Jones had ringed the barrage balloons. Then he turned to Paynter. 'Can you confirm the existence of a balloon barrage from other sources?' he asked.

'No, sir, definitely not.'

Longmore looked at the photographs again. 'You realize,' he said to Jones, 'what a serious matter this is. If I act on your word it may mean the success or failure of a very important operation. How certain are you in your own mind that there are lines of balloons in these two places?'

'I am completely certain, sir.'

'Very well, then,' said Longmore decisively, 'I will send a senior officer to Alexandria at once, to try to convince Admiral Cunningham.'

Longmore was as good as his word, and the senior officer must have succeeded in his mission, for official history records that the Swordfish pilots who launched their torpedoes at the Italian battle fleet had certainly been warned of the existence of barrage balloons.

But the photographing of the defences was not all the reconnaissance that was needed. There still had to be a final check on the position of the ships.

The morning of 10 November was still and grey at Malta, and there was hardly a ripple on the Mediterranean. At Luqa airfield the crew of one of the Marylands looked up at the blanket of low cloud.

'Ten Tenths!' exclaimed Sergeant John Spires, the navigator, in some disgust. 'How does anyone think we're going to fly to Taranto when the birds are walking and the fish are at anchor?'

The Captain of the crew, a young man of twenty-two named Pilot Officer Adrian Warburton, did not seem to be concerned about the weather.

'We're going at zero feet the whole way,' he said quietly to Spires, 'so get yourself a sharp pencil and plenty of paper. If we can't photograph, you'll have to plot the ships on the harbour map.' Then to Sergeant Moren, the gunner, he said: 'Paddy, you read the names on the sides of the ships.' In unison both sergeants expressed their feelings in a single word.

But it was all in the day's work. Off they went in 'The Sardine Tin', their somewhat battered Maryland. They crossed the stretches of dead calm sea, and then Taranto was suddenly ahead. The Italians were completely unprepared and all the balloons were down, and the Maryland flew twice round the outer harbour, Warburton trying to take photographs and Spires scribbling feverishly, before the anti-aircraft defences blazed into life. The Maryland sped out of range, and then Warburton and the other two compared notes.

'That's more than were here yesterday,' said Warburton. 'We'll have to make sure in case the photographs are no good, so we'll go in again. Now keep your peepers open. We'll check the battle-wagons together.'

He brought the Maryland down till she skimmed the water, and made straight for the curve of the harbour –

straight for the Italian fire. 'How the hell can they miss us,' thought Spires, and then concentrated with all his might on counting.

'One – two – three – four – five!' all three of them shouted. Then, 'Whacko, chaps!' called Spires. 'Let's see Warby get out of this.'

As the Maryland whistled off, an Italian biplane fighter followed after. Paddy Moren, who was itching to have a shot at it, exclaimed to Warburton, 'For crying out loud! Pull up a bit now, Warby. The so-and-so can't catch us up.'

Next day Warburton's photographs were on board the *Illustrious* – and that night the Fleet Air Arm's spectacular attack took place. But 'The Sardine Tin' had not yet finished, and on the morning after the attack Warburton and his crew took off for Taranto again to record what had happened. Spires and Moren craned to see the wreckage of the three battleships that had been hit. Oil was streaming all over the water, and large fires were burning.

'Cor – look! Bloody lovely!' 'What a prang!'

Warburton did not pay any attention to the vicious anti-aircraft fire, but just went on photographing from 6,000 feet, and it was only after a fourth run that they climbed into the cloud and made for home.

The news of the Taranto attack – 'this glorious episode' as the Prime Minister described it – resounded round the world. And meantime the *Times of Malta* ran a cartoon showing Warburton in a Maryland swooping exultantly over a battleship, while an Italian Admiral hurled his sword at him in impotent fury.

• • •

During the six months that follow Taranto, Macphail's tiny outfit at Cairo expanded into a formally established unit, No. 2 PRU, with a few more pilots and interpreters; but a slightly theatrical hush-hush atmosphere still clung to it.

In spite of the desperate shortage of aircraft in the Middle East, one or two Hurricanes were allocated to Macphail, and he had cameras fitted in them with good results. Then later Beaufighters were modified to take cameras.

It so happened that at this time Adrian Warburton was in Cairo. He was already becoming famous as the man who had photographed Taranto from fifty feet, and the first photographic pilot in the area to be awarded a DFC. He was also well known at the Captain of the Maryland crew that had shot down the most enemy planes, and who could get away with anything – as on one occasion when after photographing eight Sicilian airfields he finished up at Catania. He was so low that he was given a 'green' light from the control tower to land, and he put his undercarriage down and made a landing approach. At the crucial moment he whipped it up, and with forward guns blazing he strafed the aircraft on the tarmac, leaving two Italian torpedo-bombers and a big German transport in flames.

Warburton had been sent from Malta to Cairo for a rest from flying, but after two weeks he was posted to 2 PRU, and for a time he worked for Macphail before returning to Malta.

There is a story which has gained in the telling about the occasion on which he 'tried out' a photographic Beaufighter from the air base at Helioplis. First he flew along some of the canals near Cairo, barely above the water, photographing the barges, and pulling up sharply just before he hit them. He then decided to fly down the Cairo–Suez road to photograph a car that was coming towards him; but he failed to get any pictures as the driver of the car, seeing an aircraft approaching him at road level at 300 miles an hour, turned rapidly into the ditch. Then Warburton flew out over the desert and there he caught sight of an old Arab on a camel crossing the skyline some miles away. He flew straight over them and then looked back to see their reactions, but neither man nor beast had taken the slightest notice. Warburton turned the aircraft and proceeded to fly over them again – but with the same result. A little disappointed, he returned to Heliopolis.

•   •   •

Sir Hugh Lloyd, in his book *Briefed to Attack*, has paid tribute to Warburton and the Maryland crews, and also to the photographic interpreters who worked at Malta during the critical time he was Air Officer Commanding there. But the highest credit must be given to Lloyd himself, for the way in which he made use of photographic intelligence. His confidence in it was remarkable, and paid remarkable dividends.

When Lloyd arrived in Malta as an Air Vice-Marshal in May 1941, he had been given a clear-cut brief: his job was to assist in cutting Rommel's lifeline; in other words to help sink the Axis ships that carried supplies from Italy to North Africa. Lloyd did not hesitate. Photographic intelligence was his first and foremost need. He already had the Flight of Marylands, but there was not a single trained photographic interpreter on Malta, and he remedied this lack as quickly as possible.

The first interpreter to reach Malta from Medmenham in 1941 was Flying Officer Howard Colvin, and he was soon joined by Flying Officer Raymond Herschel, the same Ray Herschel who as a Wembley civilian had helped me to learn how to interpret aircraft. These two were amazed to find that they were to work in a tiny room opening directly off Lloyd's own office. Most of the intelligence offices were installed in underground tunnels, for Malta was already being heavily bombed, but Lloyd did not like being underground and his office was in the deep ravine-like 'ditch' that cuts through the town of Valetta. So there Colvin and Herschel set to work.

Lloyd was demanding as well as very appreciative.

'I've got to know *when* the ships are loading, *what* they are loading, and when they are going to sail,' he told the two interpreters. 'And after they've sailed I must know their course and their speed.'

This meant first of all a day-by-day watch on the port of Naples, for in 1941 the Sicilian Channel was much the most important supply route to Africa; and activity on the quays at Naples was the first sign that a convoy was soon going to leave.

One evening shortly after Herschel arrived he and Colvin were working on that day's new cover of Naples, oblivious of everything except the ships they were counting and measuring. The window of the tiny interpretation room had been boarded up because of the bombing, but a door leading immediately into 'the ditch' was usually kept open. The room was in half darkness while in front of the interpreters the desk lamps cast their circles of light.

Someone came silently in through the outside door, and a voice said to Herschel: 'Is that the new cover of Naples?'

Herschel looked up, and was aware of an RAF officer he had never seen before, fair and extremely good-looking.

'Yes – we're working on it – sir,' he answered.

'Don't "sir" me, old boy,' said Adrian Warburton.

On later occasions – Warburton got to know the interpreters very well – he used to slip into the room soundlessly in his crepe-soled desert boots; and his approach was usually announced by a flash and a thud as a huge escape knife landed on, or sometimes in, one of the desks.

Lloyd himself was always in and out when there was new cover of Naples. He wanted snap answers, and they must be right first time. This was First Phase interpretation in its purest form, stripped of every vestige of 'usual channels'. As soon as Lloyd had a verbal answer from the interpreters he acted upon it, long before a report had been sent off to Cairo.

Lloyd wanted immediate answers, and he got them. Soon Colvin and Herschel knew Naples so well, and also the little ways of the Germans and the Italians, that they could tell in a flash what was going on. The convoys were always loaded at the same spot – quickly nicknamed 'Rommel's Quay'. When a ship's hatches were battened down you could reckon she would sail within twenty-four hours (as soon as the deck cargo was aboard – the tanks, the armoured cars, the innumerable drums of oil).

So if Lloyd knew that some of the ships at 'Rommel's Quay' had their hatches on by midday, a Maryland would be off at first light the next morning to check whether they had left. Within about three hours from the moment it got back to Luqa the interpreters could say 'yes' or 'no'. If the convoy *had* left, another aircraft was sent off to find it. Once its course was known, an attack could be mounted.

This was the moment when Lloyd needed to know the speed of the ships, a fact which the photographs could tell him concisely. Colvin and Herschel merely had to refer to a formula that had been worked out earlier at Medmenham, based on the scientific theory of wave patterns, from which they could calculate the speed of a ship in knots from he spacing of the waves in its wake.

As time went on, the ships which escaped being sunk became so familiar that they were given nicknames. If Lloyd came in and suddenly said: 'Where's old Betty Martin?' Colvin knew just what he meant, and turned to his card index which recorded every movement of every ship that had ever been photographed from Malta. In a moment he could say where 'Betty Martin' had last been seen: Naples, Taranto, Brindisi, Trapani, Palermo, Messina, or Tripoli, whether she had been loading or unloading, and just whereabouts in port she had been lying.

It was largely thanks to this systematic watch – a method which was expanded at Medmenham to watch all enemy shipping – that the attacks on the North African convoys had such outstanding success. Every ship of the

Italian Navy was, of course, watched in the same way; and the devastating effect of this was frankly admitted later in the war by a leading Italian Admiral. In 1943, after Italy surrendered, he was asked why his Navy had made such a poor showing. 'No one can play chess blindfolded,' he replied. 'We never knew where the Allied Navy was. But the Allies knew the exact position of every unit of our fleet at all times.'

Until the end of 1941, the convoys that Colvin and Herschel had been tracking were usually escorted by a few destroyers; but then on 17 December Warburton came back with the news that pretty well the whole Italian fleet was escorting a convoy of four merchant ships. This was hardly an exaggeration, as Colvin found when he saw the photographs. The escort included two battleships, two cruisers, and no less than fifteen destroyers. There was no doubt that a new and a much grimmer lap of the fight against the Axis lay ahead.

Through the early months of 1942 – the height of Malta's ordeal – Warburton and the other pilots continued photographing the ports and the convoys. And since the German Air Force had returned to Sicily in strength, the watch on the airfields took on a new importance as well.

By this time Malta had a few photographic Spitfires, and regular cover of the airfields was flown at first light and last light every day. The interpreters got to know the routine at the air bases so well that any abnormality was spotted at once. At one airfield the Germans tried to fool them with dummy aircraft, but they might have spared themselves the trouble. If you are constantly watching real aircraft, a dummy stands out on a photograph like a sore thumb.

One day towards the end of April, Colvin was interpreting the airfield at Gerbini, and he was at first puzzled by some levelling that was just starting a little way from the main landing area. Subsequent covers showed other similar levellings, and each was connected with the main railway by a new spur. It certainly looked as if something was going to be brought in by rail, something for which a longish levelled strip was needed. Gliders! Ever since the German assault on Crete the year before, airborne invasion had been a haunting menace. Colvin and Herschel together took the photographs to Lloyd, and explained their theories and fears. A broad grin spread over the Air Vice-Marshal's face.

'Gliders. Gliders full of Germans,' he said. 'I hope they do come. Just let them try!'

But week after week passed and the gliders full of Germans did not come. We know now that although an airborne invasion of Malta was in fact planned, the project never matured.

It was while things were at their worst for Malta that Warburton's exploits began to create for him the reputation of a legendary hero. His natural talent for aerial photography was uncanny. The tale is told that the first time he used a camera fitted with a 36-inch lens, which demanded a higher degree of flying accuracy than the camera he was used to (since each print covers a relatively small area, at a larger scale), he photographed the port of Messina – the whole sweeping arc of it that surrounds the harbour like a question mark – on a single print.

But his persistence and his skill as a pilot were out of the ordinary as well. The story goes that once when he was photographing the Sicilian airfields in a Beaufighter, one of his engines was hit, but he finished getting his photographs before he started for home. Another time, on the way back from Sicily, without ammunition, he purposely got into a dogfight with a German and in full view of Malta manoeuvred him into the sea.

By the time that Malta's peril was over, Warburton was a Squadron Leader with a DSO and with two bars to his

DFC. He had already been jokingly called 'King of the Mediterranean', but the legend of his infallibility that was growing up was serious. He always did get his photographs. He always did fly straight through the enemy defences. He always did get back.

Admittedly, the circumstances at Malta were unique, and Warburton's personal achievements, both legendary and strictly factual, put him in an unorthodox class by himself. Nevertheless, he can be said to stand for the pilots of British photographic reconnaissance in more ways than one.

The photographic pilot has to have all the accuracy of the bomber pilot, as well as all the alertness and tactical skill of the fighter pilot. In addition, he must be an individualist who can make quick responsible decisions entirely on his own. And he must have the persistent purpose and the endurance not only to reach his target but to bring back the photographs to his base.

In all these things Warburton excelled. His achievements in his own line were quite as remarkable as those of two of the RAF's most illustrious pilots, Douglas Bader and Guy Gibson, who were both near contemporaries of his at St Edward's School, Oxford. The names of Bader and Gibson are rightly famous, but the name Adrian Warburton has hardly been heard outside the circle of those who actually knew him, and there is no single mention of him in the official RAF history of the Second World War.

●　　●　　●

Some of the pilots of PRU were destined to fly much further afield than the Mediterranean before the end of the war, and the plans that made this possible were laid in 1941. Shortly after Air Vice-Marshal Medhurst appointed Peter Stewart to organize the expansion of photographic intelligence in Britain, he sent Peter Riddell on a six-weeks' tour of the Mediterranean, the Middle East, and the Far East, to find out just what was happening and to work out a plan for the future.

Riddell flew first to Gibraltar, where he saw the few photographic Marylands that were based there, and then looked into the tiny dark cubby-hole where the interpreters worked by the light of hurricane lamps, and the former men's lavatory where the photographs were processed. Thence he went to confer with the Service chiefs, whom he found far from apathetic. But when so many 'essentials' were lacking, trimmings like photographic reconnaissance might have to be dispensed with – or so they felt.

At Malta Riddell stopped briefly, and then hurried on to Cairo. Next he flew straight to Singapore, and on the return journey visited Delhi and Simla. Back in London, he reported to Medhurst. The pattern that had been hammered out in the early days, the system of First, Second, and Third Phase interpretation and of a central inter-Service unit must be applied wherever the war had to be fought.

Less than a year later most of Riddell's recommendations had been put into effect. Very soon new high-speed photographic aircraft were flying over the sands of Africa and the jungles of Burma, and the photographs they took were being interpreted at 'little Medmenhams' in Cairo and Delhi, while at Gibraltar and Malta both the flying and the interpretation had been expanded and re-equipped. For the first time in history the watchful eye of photographic intelligence was scanning the enemy's doings all the way across the globe.

SEVEN

COMBINED OPERATIONS

In the years before Pearl Harbour there was not one single photographic interpreter in the United States Navy, and such a creature had never even been thought of. But in the spring of 1941 Vice-Admiral Ghormley, the American naval attaché in London, was so much impressed by the discoveries of the interpreters at Wembley and Medmenham that he asked for a 'competent officer' to be sent over to find out how it was done.

The officer who came over, Lieutenant Commander Robert S. Quackenbush, Jr, head of photography at the Navy's Bureau of Aeronautics, was much more than merely competent. On his first visit to Medmenham, Kendall took him on a rapid tour of all the sections, and we got a lightning glimpse of a big man full of enormous energy and liveliness, with a huge laugh and a handshake to match. Quackenbush, also known as Bob, 'Q-Bush', and 'The Godfather of Navy PI', is the sort of man who never does things by halves.

Quackenbush had three months at Medmenham, with two US Marine Corps officers, Captain Charles Cox and Captain Gooderham McCormick, who joined him to help speed up the investigation. Then, loaded with training material, he hastened back to Washington, where it took him only a few weeks to persuade the Chief of Naval Operations to let him set up a school of photographic interpretation at Anacostia. Interpreters were going to be needed – he insisted – badly needed, on every carrier in the Fleet, and at every Navy headquarters.

The school opened less than a month after Pearl Harbour, with Quackenbush, Cox, and McCormick as the teaching staff. They took special trouble to select men with the right sort of educational background, and during the first few courses they laid the foundations for the high standard of Navy interpretation which in course of time developed into a Service tradition. And Quackenbush taught his men more than how to interpret. 'No one will know beforehand why you've come, or what your work is for,' he used to tell them. 'So every Navy interpreter on ship or on shore has got to be a hell of a good salesman!'

In May 1942 Quackenbush set off again, this time to campaign for photographic intelligence in the South Pacific; but before he left there was a battle to fight in the Navy Department. He had been asked how many interpreters he needed in the South Pacific, and he said the least he could manage with was fifty. This demand was not well received, and he was summoned to the office of the Assistant Chief of Naval Operations. He argued his case from every angle, but still the senior officer was not convinced. His chief worry seemed to be that they would not have enough to do, because planes and equipment were in such short supply. Quackenbush searched desperately for some way of putting across his urgent conviction.

'In the Fire Department,' he burst out, 'the men have nothing to do for days on end, and they sit around playing cards and loafing. But when there's a fire you're glad they're there.'

It worked, and after a moment's silence the answer came: 'Okay, I'll give them to you.'

In those early days after Pearl Harbour, the battle which Quackenbush had to fight, and fought with relish, was a very straightforward affair compared to the 'cold war' that had to be waged by the champions of photographic intelligence in the US Army Air Corps. But in both Services a completely new idea had to be introduced with the greatest possible speed, and it was bound to be a struggle.

Only a short time previously no one in the Air Corps, any more than in the Navy, had an inkling of what the new photographic intelligence meant; and when, in the summer of 1941, an officer named Captain Harvey C. Brown, Jr, was assigned to England for a 'photographic course', he gathered that he was being sent to study the latest developments in British camera techniques. He soon discovered he was on the track of something quite different.

In September 1941, when Kendall brought to my section a lanky American captain, with a poker face and a Virginian drawl, and asked me to explain to him what I was doing, I was delighted to tell him about my work. I was in the thick of my first major investigation for the Air Ministry, on the subject of German gliders. There were fears that the Germans might try to stage an airborne invasion of Britain, and the Air Ministry had been called upon to estimate the extent of the threat. By this time I had a most reliable helper, Charles Sims, who before the war had been chief photographer to *The Aeroplane*, and together we rushed out a big report on gliders in just over a week.

'This is their standard troop-carrying glider, the DFS 230,' I explained to Captain Brown as I showed him photographs of the gliders at Maleme during the invasion of Crete. 'And here, you see, they used the same type last year to land troops inside the Belgian fort at Eben-Emael when they were overrunning the Low Countries. That was the first time we ever saw them.'

'Why do they look so white and flat?' he asked.

'That's because they aren't camouflage-painted,' I told him, 'so their surface reflects the light. They aren't actually as big as they look. We have to allow for that when we're measuring them.'

'Why do you have to measure them if you've recognized the type already?'

'Oh, we're always on the look-out for modifications,' I replied. 'You see, there's a great deal we want to find out about these gliders. We want to make sure how many types there are, and how many men they will carry.'

'So I suppose you measure the wing-span of a German soldier and then figure out how many can be packed in.' Harvey Brown's expression was deadly serious, but there was a flicker of a smile and I was a bit annoyed.

'No; we don't do any load calculations here. It's our job to give all the dimensions we can, especially the wing-span and the root chord. Then Flight Lieutenant Golovine at the Air Ministry, who knows what wing loadings are likely for big gliders, works out an estimate of what they can carry.'

Harvey Brown seemed suitably impressed, and I produced more photographs.

'Have a look at this.' I pointed to three of the Germans' mammoth new troop-carriers. 'A wing-span of 178 feet. It's more than double the size of anything we've seen before. Golovine says it could carry a small tank.'

I put my treasured Leitz magnifier in position and Brown bent to look.

'This is a swell little gadget,' he said. 'Where did you get it?'

I laughed. 'It was the last pre-war German magnifier in London. I was very lucky indeed.'

'It's doing a good job of work for the fatherland. And how close can you get with your measurements?'

'Oh, it all depends on the photographs. But on good pictures we reckon on getting within a couple of feet of wing-span. Length is much more tricky, because you can't see exactly where the tail unit ends; and the nose may be deceptive too. We measure every single photograph of every glider that's seen, so from an average of our figures the Air Ministry can make pretty accurate estimates.'

Brown pondered over this. 'If Goering knew how much

you're finding out,' he said, 'it sure would send his wing loading up.'

No wonder Harvey Brown was fascinated, and as he visited all the sections at Medmenham one after another he became fired with a burning faith in what photographic intelligence could do. He determined to spread the gospel on his return. But when he did get back to America he found himself up against a considerable amount of prejudice.

Between the wars, aerial photography had meant one thing and one thing only in the Air Corps: mapping; and there was good reason for this. In the twenties, when photography was first being tried out seriously for peacetime mapping, only a tiny fraction of the vast continent of America had been accurately mapped, and the Army's Corps of Engineers jumped at the chance to begin tackling the work in this rapid economical manner. Over the years the technique of mapping photography was much improved, and the Tri-Metrogon system, with three synchronized cameras taking photographs from horizon to horizon, was widely adopted.

This mapping was, of course, an enterprise involving the Air Corps as well as the Corps of Engineers; and just before America came into the Second World War one of the leading figures in it was an Air Corps officer named Major Minton W. Kaye. General Arnold had come to place much confidence in him, so the view that mapping was the sole function of aerial photography pervaded the highest councils of the Air Corps.

In some quarters, however, complete and utter ignorance prevailed as to the potentialities of aerial photographs, even for mapping. Brigadier General George W. Goddard, one of the great pioneers of aerial photography in the US, who was then a Major and in charge of photographic experiments at Wright Field, was constantly meeting this lack of understanding. There is an apocryphal story that in the thirties, when he was engaged on a mapping project in the Philippines, an Army officer came to see him one day and said he wanted to inspect the dark-room. Goddard showed him round, wondering; and the officer took the prints out of the processing tanks, looked at them one by one, grunted, and finally seemed content. Then he told Goddard why he had come. Apparently at another photographic unit in General MacArthur's domain the processing tanks had been found full of pictures of nude women! Goddard took the opportunity to interest the officer in his mapping work and as a result he was shortly afterwards honoured by a visit from MacArthur himself. The General arrived in riding-kit, with boots so shiny that you could see them a mile away, and asked Goddard what he was doing. Goddard said he was making maps and showed him a photographic mosaic.

MacArthur looked at it askance, tapped it with his riding-crop, and said: 'Since when has that been a map?'

'According to Webster's Dictionary, sir,' answered Goddard, 'a map is a representation of the surface of the earth, and *this*' – his eyes lit up – 'has no human errors.'

MacArthur glowered, and his aide nudged Goddard to warn him to stop. Various other photographs were discussed, and the General turned to go. As he went out he pointed to the offending mosaic, and snapped at Goddard: 'You understand, that's not a map!'

With this sort of background it is hardly surprising that the good news Harvey Brown brought back from Medmenham received little immediate response. When he reached Washington, some of his superiors in intelligence, including Lieutenant Colonel Lauris Norstad, were very much interested; but further afield he got cynical smiles and no encouragement at all. Little by little, however, during the chaotic weeks and months after Pearl Harbour, the importance of the new branch of intelligence was recognized.

It was in March 1942, while the Japs swept on southwards and the battle continued grimly in Europe, that the Army Air Forces Intelligence School was started up at Harrisburg in Pennsylvania, under the direction of Colonel Egmont Koenig. It was a major innovation: before Pearl Harbour, intelligence of all kinds had been seriously neglected. Soon after the training courses began, one of the instructors wrote to a friend in Washington:

> Colonel Koenig is doing a terrific job, and the school is indispensable. We must insure that it continues after the war, so that never again will we find ourselves at the beginning of another conflict so completely dependent for intelligence on the RAF Air Ministry and on the editors of *Time*, *Life*, and *Fortune!!*

The main purpose of the school was to train new arrivals from civilian life as air intelligence officers, and photographic interpretation was the subject of one of the brief specialist courses. Harvey Brown joined the staff, first as an instructor and among his colleagues who helped to develop 'PI' were Major F. Martin Brown and Captain Samuel L. Batchelder, who later held important operational assignments. They were all enthusiasts, and so were their pupils on the early courses – handpicked men including a number of peacetime architects.

But unfortunately the policy of careful selection was abandoned before long. Washington's full approval and acceptance of photographic intelligence, when it finally came, took a very unfortunate form. A concept of mass production was imposed from on high, and classes of literally hundreds of men, many of them not in the least interested in interpretation or suitable for the work, had to be herded through the school.

By this time, however, the first Harrisburg graduates had joined the advance guard of the Eighth Air Force in England. In June 1942 some of them attended

Medmenham's school of interpretation at Nuneham Courtenay in Oxfordshire; and it was in August that a small group of American interpreters, led by Captain Marvin B. Sterling, entered the precincts of Danesfield, bringing with them 'PI kits' suitable for starting operations on a desert island. From then on, as more and more Americans came over from Harrisburg, Medmenham began to be transformed into a completely Allied unit.

•   •   •

In the summer of 1942, when the plans for the North African landings were being worked out, photographic intelligence was called upon to provide a mass of material for planning and briefing. This was an undertaking far bigger and more complicated than anything of its kind that had been tackled before.

A great deal of special photography was done, both from Gibraltar and Malta, and then Medmenham hurried to work on models and topographical reports. These were needed so that the landings could be followed up with precise purpose, and General Eisenhower's planners wanted to know every detail: the width and condition of the roads, the dimensions of the airfields, exact details of the defences, the heights of buildings, the positions of pylons and telephone posts.

It fell to Douglas Kendall to direct the project, as he was responsible for the immediate operational work at Medmenham. Some months earlier he had found that there was a steady demand for very detailed interpretations of pin-points 'on the other side', so that agents who were going to land by parachute or by boat could be properly briefed. They needed a lot of facts that no map could give: the height of a hedge round a farmhouse, the position of barbed wire, the low-water line of a creek – knowledge of these might easily mean the difference between success and failure. So Kendall took two of his interpreters off Second Phase work to give all their time to this. When the prospect of the North African landings loomed up, however, the cosy little section had to be tremendously expanded; no easy matter on the spur of the moment. But Kendall managed to collect an inter-Allied, inter-Service team which included Americans, Canadians, Navy, Army, and RAF officers; and also two recently commissioned WAAFs, Dorothy Garrod and Sarah Oliver, or, as most people thought of her, Sarah Churchill – the daughter of the Prime Minister.

Dorothy Garrod, before she joined the WAAF, was Professor of Archaeology at Cambridge and an eminent authority on her subject. It was second nature to her to search patiently, and to piece together not only the obvious findings but the puzzling chance discoveries that are sometimes just as significant. Sarah, who brightened the scene with her glamour and elegance and wit, was a quick and versatile interpreter, and adept at relating air photographs to maps: before she became an officer she had been a Medmenham plotter. During the hectic weeks that Kendall's team laboured on the reports that contributed so much to the success of *Operation Torch*, she pulled her weight with enthusiasm, like all the others.

On 7 November, after the rush at Medmenham was all over, Sarah went off to Chequers on 48-hour leave, and late that evening she and her father were alone together. It was nearly 1.0 a.m.; Sarah was curled up in a big chair by the fire, and Churchill was pacing up and down. Then the clock struck.

'At this very minute', announced Churchill with measured gravity; 'at this very minute; under cover of darkness; the six hundred and forty-three ships that are carrying our troops on their great enterprise are approaching the shores of Africa.'

'Six hundred and forty-four,' said a voice from the armchair.'

'What's that?'

'I've been working on *Torch* for months.'

'Why didn't you tell me?'

'I was told not to mention it to anyone.'

Her father smiled.

'S'pose you thought I didn't know,' was his last word.

While the second daughter of the British Prime Minister worked away as an interpreter at Medmenham, the second son of the President of the United States was helping to build up photographic reconnaissance in the Army Air Forces.

In the summer of 1942, Lieutenant Colonel Elliott Roosevelt was put in command of the 3rd Reconnaissance Group, the first American unit of its kind to be sent over to Europe. The Group had two squadrons of Lightnings – twin-boom fighter aircraft equipped with cameras instead of guns – and a squadron of Flying Fortress bombers modified for mapping photography.

For Elliott Roosevelt, the command of a Group which was to take part in operations was a stimulating development in his Air Force career. He had been occupied with aerial photography for nearly two years already, but it had all been mapping and survey: first of all finding sites for North Atlantic air bases, and then early in 1942 in West Africa, mapping certain areas that were important to the Vichy French. So Elliott brought to photographic reconnaissance a specialized variety of technical experience, but of course he brought much else besides – including publicity.

The 3rd Reconnaissance Group was based for a short time in England, and while it was there Mrs Roosevelt came over on a visit to Britain. It was arranged that she should drive down from London to visit Elliott's unit at Steeple Morden in Cambridgeshire. There is a famous story about how her driver got lost, and when they asked the way no one would tell them. So finally, when they were nearly an hour late, her escort phoned back to the American Embassy for instructions, and as 'Rover' was the code name for Mrs Roosevelt during her visit, he announced dramatically over the telephone: 'Rover has lost her pup.' Eventually she got to Steeple Morden, however, just before it was too dark to see anything.

• • •

During the crucial days after the North African landings, while the 3rd Reconnaissance Group awaited the signal to join General Doolittle's Twelfth Air Force in Africa, there was urgent photography to be done by the US Navy.

On board the aircraft carrier USS *Ranger*, as she rode the Atlantic waves off Casablanca, a young officer who was one of the photographic interpreters assigned to the air support force for the Moroccan landings rescued some photographs that were slithering across the table. He put the prints back in order, ready at hand to compare with the new shots of Casablanca harbour that would be through from processing at any moment. It was 10 November 1942, the second day after the landings began.

He had never set foot in Casablanca in his life, but he knew the port so well from photographs that he felt he could have found his way blindfold to the Môle du Commerce, where the newest battleship of the French Navy, *Jean Bart*, lay uncompleted but defiant. On those amazing pictures that one of the British aces from Gibraltar had taken at roof-top level you could see there were no guns in the after positions, and one of the forward turrets was not finished either. But the other forward turret was very much complete. The four slim grey pencils that pointed seaward were 15-inch guns that only two days earlier had started firing murderous salvoes at the invasion fleet – until they were silenced by answering fire from the *Massachusetts*. Since then the carrier-based dive-bombers had been at work, and nothing more had been heard from *Jean Bart*. It seemed that the Vichy French resistance was almost over now. Across the water the cruiser *Augusta*, Admiral Hewitt's flagship, was moving in. The new pictures that the Ranger's photographic plane had just taken would show exactly how much damage the dive-bombers had done, but at this stage it seemed a bit academic.

Ah! The photos. The Ensign shuffled through them quickly and picked out a couple of prints. *There* she is, the long slim shape that dwarfs all the other shipping, with her booms round her like a two-stranded necklace of beads. And the guns? One glance was enough. He blenched and leapt to his feet. The guns had *not* been damaged by the dive-bombers, so they might very well be ready for action by now. And the *Augusta* was steaming within range.

Snatching the photographs, he tore up to the bridge. But barely had an agonized message been radioed to Admiral Hewitt when there came the shriek of approaching shells. Just ahead of the flagship two geysers of yellow-dyed water leapt sixty feet into the air, drenching the Admiral and all the officers on the bridge. This was the first of eleven two-gun salvoes from *Jean Bart* that straddled the American flagship as she hastily retreated.

After that the dive-bombers from the Ranger really did finish off those guns; but they say that from then on Admiral Hewitt always set great store by photographic intelligence.

Only a few days after this, reconnaissance was starting up from a North African base. A unit of Spitfires from Benson, No. 4 PRU, which had been waiting at Gibraltar, flew to Algiers on 13 November and began operating from the airfield at Maison Blanche. Their first objectives were the airfields and quays of Tunis and Bizerta, as the Germans were already pouring troops and supplies into Tunisia. But Maison Blanche was being bombed often and hard, and when the first arrivals of Elliott Roosevelt's Group – the mapping Fortresses – got there a few days later, the field was strewn with smashed aircraft, including most of the photographic Spitfires. There was urgent need for news of the German movements, so it was decided that Lieutenant Colonel James Anderson, the Group's operations officer, should set off in one of the Fortresses and make a photographic tour of Tunisia. This was a fine chance for American 'PR' to prove itself.

The following morning Anderson took off from Maison Blanche with Major Wayne Thurman as co-pilot. He set course for Kasserine and there he dropped down to 6,000 feet, turned on his cameras, and made several long runs over the wilderness between the hills with the solitary road winding along it. Then he climbed eastwards and made three runs over Gabes; then trundled on northwards up the coast and finally back to Algiers, landing safely after seven and a half hours' flying. There had not been a single sign of enemy opposition.

But then a problem arose: how were the films to be processed? The newly arrived RAF photographic section had been bombed out a couple of nights before. Anderson discovered, however, that they had managed to get going again temporarily in a factory some miles away. So off he went to the factory and sought out the photographic officer, Flight Lieutenant Walton – the very man who as a sergeant had kept things going in the trailers at Tigeaux at the time of the fall of France.

Walton and his men were working under extremely primitive conditions, with hardly any proper equipment. The films were being thumb-tacked to broom handles and wound through the developer by hand. There was no way of washing them adequately, and the smell of hypo nearly knocked you down. Nor was there any drying machinery, and the wet films were being hung out to dry, draped from lathe to lathe in the machine-shops.

Next morning Anderson came back to collect his films.

They were still somewhat damp, but he took them straight to the Twelfth Air Force headquarters in Algiers. The intelligence officer he found there was quite excited about them, and not at all worried by the lack of an interpretation report. Some interpreters were supposed to be on the way from Harrisburg, but there hadn't been a sign of them yet. What did it matter? The thing that mattered was that the targets had been photographed. The General must see them.

Before Anderson knew what was happening he was being escorted into the presence of General Doolittle, and called upon to make a running commentary on his own photographs. For the better part of an hour the films were unreeled in turn, and before the end of it the General himself was pointing things out to Anderson. Thus took place the interpretation of the first American photographic sortie flown over the North African battleground.

That unchallenged flight of Anderson's – before the German defences were in shape – was unfortunately not a precedent; and during the first few months in North Africa the 3rd Reconnaissance Group lost more than twenty-five per cent of its original pilots. The winter of 1942 was a time of sad misfortune for American 'recce', as it was for the Air Forces and Armies it served, and of lessons hardly learned. Many of the pilots were men who had wanted to be in fighters, and resented having been switched to what they considered a 'sissy' job, and their discontent was aggravated by the fact that the early photographic Lightning was not really suitable for its task. At low levels, for dicing, it was swift and successful; but on the normal high-level sorties it could not outpace the enemy fighters – it wallowed about and was 'duck soup for the 109s'. It was also nicely within range of the German flak.

The American interpreters were in a bad way too.

When the men from Harrisburg arrived on the scene they were installed in a schoolhouse in Algiers, several miles from the British interpreters who worked in another schoolhouse at Maison Carrée, which was in turn many miles from the airfield. The unhappy Americans, confronted for the first time with photographs of the strange African desert, looked, and measured, and checked with their recognition charts, and looked again, and then sent out their reports hoping for the best. But sometimes they were very wide of the mark, as for instance when they found a convoy of enemy tanks which had apparently turned up from nowhere. Bing! Out went the report, and the British First Army, which was accustomed to rely on photographic intelligence, swung into appropriate action. Meantime, however, the sensational news had reached Maison Carrée, and the head RAF interpreter decided to have a look at the most recent British photographs of the spot where the 'convoy' had been found. To someone who knows what to expect in the desert, and knows that a convoy of tanks cannot move without making tracks that nothing can hide, it was incredible – scandalous – that a convoy of camels resting should have been mistaken for a convoy of tanks. Out went a British signal immediately: 'For tanks read camels' – but the story goes that units of the First Army had already moved sixty miles.

Such was the inevitable result of working 'independently'. At this point there was no official coordination between the American and British interpreters, and the miles that separated them made even unofficial liaison difficult.

The British were having their troubles too, and lack of continuity between the flying and the processing and interpreting meant that sometimes 'immediate' reports were not actually issued till forty-eight hours after the photographs were taken. Fortunately, however, the creation of a Mediterranean Air Command in February

1943 led to the amalgamation of the British and American photographic units in North Africa. Elliott Roosevelt, promoted to Colonel, was put in command of the new Allied Wing, with Eric Fuller – by this time a Wing Commander and one of the outstanding organizers in photographic intelligence – as his deputy. From then on both the flying and the interpretation were completely integrated, and there was also a great expansion to keep pace with the growing demand for photographs.

In the spring of 1943 the main responsibility of the new Wing was to serve as eyes for the Allied Armies that were closing in on Tunis. But there was also another big undertaking which was of special interest to Elliott Roosevelt with his early experience of mapping. Sicily was to be mapped, in preparation for the next move after Tunis was secured. So an extensive programme of mapping flights was started up from Algiers and Malta.

The pilots who were sent to fly their Lightnings from Malta were the first of the Americans to come into touch with Adrian Warburton and to fall under his spell. When he came out to greet them at Luqa airfield, wearing old grey flannels with a battledress tunic, and a forage cap shoved on to his blonde hair, he had just 'returned from the dead' after being posted missing for three days. It was a fantastic story – a typical Warburton story. He had been photographing Bizerta when his plane was disabled by flak, but he managed to struggle on as far as Bone, and somehow landed without hurt. There he was kept under lock and key for two days, suspected of being a German agent. But in the end he established that he was British, and was given a French plane to fly on to Gibraltar. There he changed it for a Spitfire, and finally flew back to Malta, picking up his cameras and films at Bone, and shooting down a Ju 88 on the way. When at last he landed at Malta, his first remark was – allegedly – 'Sorry I'm late.'

Squadron Leader Warburton, as the Americans called him at first, was soon just 'Warby'; and the things he could do in a Lightning made them feel that perhaps it wasn't such a bad ship after all. Before long Warburton was attached to the American Group; and so from Malta he came to Tunis, to the air base at La Marsa which became the home of the photographic Wing. But he was always back and forth – in typical Warburton fashion. On one occasion he had just taken off from La Marsa in a Lightning when it began to give trouble, and he had to crash-land. He leapt clear of the aircraft, and a moment later the cockpit was a roaring mass of flames; but within twenty minutes Warburton had borrowed another Lightning.

A little crowd gathered to gaze aghast at the blazing aircraft, and they asked one another in horror: 'Where's the pilot? Did he get out?'

One of the American pilots, Major John Hoover, pointed upwards to a plane that was fast disappearing in the direction of Malta. 'There he is,' he explained to the incredulous onlookers.

• • •

For six months the Wing worked from Tunis – from June to December 1943 – at a tempo that steadily increased, for the Army commanders were coming to realize more and more that photography was as indispensable to them as air support. Before, and during, and after the assault on Sicily, and again when the time came for the invasion of Italy itself, the interpreters kept constant track of the enemy's doings: on the roads and at the ports, at the airfields, and at the marshalling yards. This intelligence was coordinated at the interpretation headquarters near La Marsa, but First Phase interpreters accompanied the detached flights of photographic aircraft that went ahead with the armies.

At Tunis there was also much targeting and damage assessment to be done. Before 19 July 1943, the date of the historic bombing attack on the Rome marshalling yards and airfields, a target map of the city had to be prepared, and the photographs of three successive flights over Rome were combined to form a mosaic which was quite a new line in target maps. Four points – the Vatican City and three famous churches – were marked with prominent warnings: MUST ON NO ACCOUNT BE DAMAGED. The crews of the bombers that took part in the big attack were briefed with the greatest care, and each man was given a copy of the photographic map. But nevertheless, the damage assessment sortie was one of the most anxiously awaited of the whole war. When Squadron Leader Morgan took off for Rome in his Spitfire, only a few hours after the attack itself, there were other aircraft standing by in case he did not return. But Morgan did return, with photographs that showed precision bombing of the highest order. Before the next morning the whole world knew that the two main marshalling yards had been put out of action, and there was much damage at the airfields, but that in the whole of the city only one religious shrine – the Basilica of San Lorenzo – had received any damage.

While the photography from Tunis continued apace, Elliott Roosevelt was summoned to Washington to help in planning a vast expansion of photographic reconnaissance. Back at La Marsa in October he called a meeting of American officers and told them of great things to come; there would be opportunities for promotion all along the line. The other excitement was that Lieutenant-Colonel Karl Polifka, who had accompanied him from Washington, was to take a leading part in the new set-up. 'Pop' Polifka was already a renowned figure – a photographic pilot who could 'do anything', and also a fine organizer and leader. As a regular Air Corps officer he had been taking photographs for mapping before Pearl Harbour, and then early in 1942 he had commanded the first unit of photographic Lightnings, which operated from Australia.

Soon Elliott was off again; this time to Cairo and Teheran for the Conferences. But just before he left, on 20 November 1943, there was a historic occasion at Tunis.

President Roosevelt, on his way to the Cairo Conference from America, broke his journey at Tunis. Elliott met him at the airfield and drove with him to the villa where he was staying – only ten minutes from La Marsa. It was a wonderful chance, and Elliott seized it. In his book *As He Saw It* he has described the conversation with his father.

'Would you, Pop?'

'What's that?'

'Inspect my units at La Marsa.'

'Sure! When? Could we tuck it in later this afternoon? Say around five o'clock?'

Late that afternoon, against the dramatic setting of a Tunisian sunset, the review took place. A jeep bearing the President, accompanied by Generals Eisenhower and Spaatz, followed by General Arnold in a staff car, passed slowly along the line and stopped when it reached Elliott. Polifka and Fuller were presented, and father and son shook hands.

'See the uniforms, Pop? We've got a regular United Nations, right here.'

'Americans, of course. French, British, Canadians . . . what's that uniform?'

'South African. And there are New Zealanders and Australians, too.'

'Looks like a fine outfit, Elliott. You should be proud.'

'Don't worry. I am.'

Two months later, early in 1944, Elliott Roosevelt was busy with new projects in England, and Polifka had taken over command of the huge new Allied set-up in the Mediterranean area. With the advance into Italy, the main base for photographic reconnaissance was established near Foggia. Almost every other building in the shabby provincial town of San Severo was taken over, and the Spitfires and Mosquitos and Lightnings operated from the nearby airfield.

In numbers the organization was primarily American, but it still depended to a great extent on British experience and skill, particularly in interpretation. On the flying side the Americans were fast developing along their own lines, as improved Lightnings came into service and the pilots began to take to the idea of photographic reconnaissance.

'Pop' Polifka was an inspiring leader during the long-drawn-out months when so many things seemed to go wrong in Italy; when inevitably there was a longing to get finished and get home. Cheery, forceful, tireless, he was always dashing off in his Lightning *Rosebud* to see his squadrons at their forward bases, or to the Air Force headquarters at Naples, or to Algiers, or England for conferences. When he crossed the Apennines he used to swoop down the valleys, setting the boulders in the stream beds rolling; and on one occasion, when he took Fuller out over the Adriatic for a 'pick-a-back' flight (which meant cramming the two of them into the single-seat cockpit), he remarked casually: 'Tell me, Eric, are we making a good wake?'

Polifka was thirty-three, allegedly too old for operational flying, so when he went on sorties he used to enter himself in the records as Lieutenant Jones. Perhaps the most famous photographs he ever took were of the valleys either side of Cassino, from the same level as the flak on the hillsides. They say that when Polifka's General saw the pictures he called for Lieutenant Jones to congratulate him, and started writing out a citation. When Polifka appeared with a sheepish grin, the General and he both thoroughly enjoyed the joke.

There was quite a bit of rivalry between Polifka and one of his Group commanders, Lieutenant Colonel Leon Gray, as to which could take the maddest risks. Polifka could usually set the pace, in tall stories as well as in actual achievements. But Leon Gray once came back from a mission claiming that two German fighters had positioned to attack him, one from either side, so he manoeuvred exactly between them, then nipped smartly out of the way, and – wham! – the two Germans met in one terrific crash.

EIGHT

THE ALLIED BOMBING OFFENSIVE

At RAF Bomber Command, during the later years of the war, photographic intelligence gradually became accepted as indispensable, both for planning operations and for assessing their results. The days when many at Bomber Command frankly disbelieved the photographs were over; reports from Medmenham were no longer unwelcome (as long as they were worded with tact), and the stream of distinguished visitors to Sir Arthur Harris's house were all in due course led into the 'conversion room', where they were shown photographs of the devastated German cities in an instrument called a steropticon – irreverently nicknamed by some 'Harris's juke box'. So the climate had changed considerably since the beginning of the war.

But it was not only as an aid to targeting and damage assessment that photographic intelligence assisted Bomber Command. Medmenham was also helping to find out the esoteric secrets of the Germans' counter-measures; and the story of how Squadron Leader Claude Wavell and his section tracked down the inventions of German radar is as exciting as a detective novel.

It all started back at Wembley, when a young scientist named Dr R.V. Jones, one of Churchill's advisers on 'the Wizard War', came out to 'Paduoc House' in connection with cover of a certain point on the French coast where a beam transmitter was suspected. He and Wavell at once made friends, and from then on a close partnership grew up, with Wavell giving almost his entire time to this special work, while Jones briefed him and followed up his reports. It was one of Wavell's discoveries, combined with the daring and skill of a leading photographic pilot, which led up to the famous Commando raid on Bruneval.

The distance of fifteen miles that separated Medmenham from the airfield at Benson was a gulf that was not very often crossed, which was a great pity. Whenever any of us did go over to meet the pilots, or when, during spells of bad weather, some of the pilots came over to Medmenham, it always left one feeling 'why can't this happen more often?' Both our work and the pilots' seemed to get a tremendous boost from it.

Gordon Hughes was one of the pilots who came over most often and he brought others along with him, to browse one afternoon, during the first winter at Medmenham, he dropped in to see Claude Wavell and to look at an instrument which Wavell had himself designed and made for measuring heights on air photographs.

'Yes, I've called it the Altazimeter,' said Wavell as he displayed the beautiful gadget that looked like a globe made of concentric circles of wood. 'We have to measure more heights than any other section, partly for analysing the installations we find, and also to provide low-flying information for the operations people. And this saves a tremendous lot of time; each calculation takes only a few minutes instead of more than thirty. This is the formula if you're interested: height equals shadow-length times the tangent of the sun's altitude; so the only data you need are latitude, the scale of the photographs, the orientation, and the date. The Altazimeter does the rest. It's as much a time saver as a slide-rule, and it's merely an application of the simple principles of spherical trigonometry.'

Then Wavell suddenly put the Altazimeter aside.

'Look here,' he said, 'I've got something else that will interest you.' He produced a pair of photographs showing a bit of French coastline, with an isolated house near the edge of high cliffs.

'We're on the lookout for a new radio direction-finding apparatus; and there's something near this house that's very suspicious, but you can't tell on this cover. The scale's too small.'

Gordon Hughes looked through Wavell's stereoscope and agreed that the scale was too small.

'There!' Wavell pointed to a minute speck near the isolated house. 'I think it may be a paraboloidal installation.'

Gordon examined the speck, and wondered how on earth one could even guess that it was a paraboloidal installation; but Wavell should know. Then he suddenly remembered he had to meet another pilot who had come over with him from Benson. He jumped to his feet.

'Sorry – wish I could stay a bit longer, but Tony Hill's downstairs and he'll be waiting for me.'

'Tell him to come and have a look at this,' said Wavell.

Gordon was back in a few minutes with Tony Hill. 'What's all the excitement about?' asked Hill, nodding his head in mock seriousness. 'Gordon and I ought to be off on a beer-tasting expedition by now.'

Wavell explained, and showed the small-scale prints to Hill. Then he brought over some low-level photographs and became quite animated as he described what Dr Jones had discovered of the Germans' methods from earlier interpretations.

'Remember these? The obliques that Manifould took of Auderville? That was the very first German RDF array on the French coast. See the two rotating frame aerials? The first clue was on small-scale cover; you couldn't see the frames themselves at all, but we got a lead because on consecutive prints, taken nine seconds apart, you could see first a thin shadow and then a thick one. That strongly suggested that a thin framework was rotating. It was so important that Dr Jones got a low-level sortie laid on. Sergeant Parrott tried first and his photographs tended to confirm our suspicions. Then six days later Flying Officer Manifould went over, and took these. Really splendid, aren't they? And, d'you know, they arrived the very night before an important meeting in London. You can just imagine the excitement when Dr Jones produced them. There had been reports that the Germans were using RDF, but this was the first proof.'

Hill had dropped his bantering manner, and was gazing through Wavell's stereoscope at the pair of prints.

'Where exactly is this place?' he asked.

'It's Cap d'Antifer, near Le Havre,' answered Wavell, 'and the little village there is called Bruneval.' Then he laughed and turned on the two DFCs, pretending to be angry. 'You pilots annoy me. You go in over this place time and time again and never turn on your cameras soon enough!'

'I'll get you the answer tomorrow,' replied Tony Hill.

The next day Wavell saw on the board ETRETAT – HILL. So he *was* after Bruneval. Wavell knew only too well how strong the anti-aircraft defences were and he was restless till news came through of Hill's return. Then he phoned him at Benson and asked: 'What's it like?'

'Like an electric bowl-fire,' said Hill, 'and about ten feet across.'

From then on the new German RDF apparatus was universally known as 'the Bowl-fire'. 'I could see it quite well,' went on Hill, 'but my camera packed up; so I'll have another go tomorrow.'

Although it was an unwritten law that you never flew the same dicing sortie two days running, because the whole idea of dicing was surprise, there was no stopping Tony Hill once he made up his mind. Next day he did return to Bruneval, and brought back 'close-ups' taken from so low that you could see into the ground floor windows of the steep-roofed house near the radar installation.

That was the sort of thing that Tony Hill always did do – right to the end. A year later – by which time he was Squadron Leader Hill, DSO, DFC – he went out to dice several targets near Le Creusot, but had camera trouble. 'I'll go again,' he said; and as it was Tony Hill, he went. This time the defences were waiting for him and shot him down to his death.

Really good low obliques are a most compelling form of intelligence, and Tony Hill's magnificent photographs played a big part in bringing about the Bruneval raid. But the detailed planning that was necessary could not be done from photographs alone, however good, and it was at this point that one of Medmenham's most secret departments – the Model Making Section – had to step in. The work of the model makers, which contributed vitally to the planning of innumerable operations all through the war, was far from a merely mechanical task. They interpreted the photographs just as much as all the rest of us, but they translated them into a different language: into solid three-dimensional replicas instead of into written reports.

At the time the Bruneval raid was being planned the cellars of Danesfield were the setting for this highly secret activity. There Flight Lieutenant Geoffrey Deeley, a peace-time sculptor, worked with a staff of specialists – many of them also sculptors or artists. There they studied all the photographs of the area they could lay hands on, and with fret-saw and spatula and paintbrush they gradually brought to life – in precise miniature – the whole setting for the raid.

The Model Section was full of the whir of electric fret-saws and the tapping of hammers as the contours that had been traced from greatly enlarged maps were cut out of hardboard one after another, and then mounted and nailed into position. Next, after being smoothed by electric chisel, the land form was given an unbroken surface with a special plastic substance, and after this had set an enormously enlarged photograph, damped to make it supple, was pushed gently into place. Thus the towering cliffs of Cap d'Antifer were given their height, and the little valley near Bruneval its gentle slope. Finally the model was painted in the sombre colours of the winter landscape, and the model makers set in place with tweezers the Lilliputian buildings and trees and fences and, of course, 'the Bowl-fire' itself. Anything over three feet high was shown three-dimensionally, and if you stooped down and looked along the surface of the model you could see exactly what the Commandos were going to encounter. This was the very model that the troops and aircrews studied with infinite care before the raid on the night of 27 February 1942 when essential parts of the installation were successfully captured.

During the following year Claude Wavell discovered that the Germans had produced a much bigger variety of 'Bowl-fire': paraboloids twenty feet across were being set up in groups of three. This new type of installation was made of metal trellis work, so it was promptly named 'the Basket'; and Wavell suddenly remembered that the Zeppelin airships had a framework constructed on the same principle. He also knew that there had recently been reports of secret war production at the Zeppelin works at Friedrichshafen, near the Swiss border. Putting two and two together, he rushed to examine the latest photographs of Friedrichshafen, and to his delight he found outside the factory stacks of components resembling 'the Basket'. Moreover they were evidently being used, for the stacks varied in shape from cover to cover.

This discovery was made early in June 1943, and on 14 June, Whit Monday, Winston Churchill paid a visit to Medmenham, accompanied by Mrs Churchill. In each department the interpreters were amazed at Churchill's detailed knowledge of their subject and his appreciation of their techniques.

Claude Wavell showed him the photographs of the Zeppelin factory, and told him what was happening there, upon which he turned to Mrs Churchill and explained to her just how the German radiolocation system worked. Then he said to Wavell: 'Have we been there yet?' Wavell replied that the factory had not so far been attacked. Churchill made no comment and continued his tour. Six days later sixty Lancasters made a daring and successful raid on the Zeppelin works.

When my own turn came I was ready with my best enlargements of German aircraft, and I was prepared to explain them, as was often necessary to distinguished visitors. But there was no need to explain to Churchill. Instead we discussed the aircraft as fellow specialists. He was about to go when he gave me rather a piercing look, and asked if I were any relation of Henry Babington Smith. When I said, 'Yes, he was my father,' he shook hands and said, 'I knew him well.' They had met long ago in India, when my father was Private Secretary to the Viceroy.

The Churchills continued their tour and reached the Night Photograph section. My brother Bernard, who was in charge, was also ready to make explanations, and also found they were not needed.

●　　●　　●

The work of the Night Photograph Section at Medmenham was a development from Bernard's early researches at Oakington. But by 1943, when all the night bombers were equipped with cameras, the detailed interpretation of their photographs was a vast undertaking, and the section at Medmenham increased in size accordingly. After the big raids there were always scores of rolls of film to be examined – Barnard had found that negatives showed quite a lot more detail than prints.

With more and more films to work on, it became possible to piece together the story of each attack by analysing what had been happening on the ground. One discovery of outstanding importance was that the development of a raid could be deduced from the pattern in which the incendiaries had fallen, and the position of fires that had been started. This information, in the form of 'fire plots', was of considerable interest to those concerned with planning, especially the Operational Research Section at Bomber Command.

But probably the most important of all the work that Medmenham did for Bomber Command was the assessment of damage from day photographs. This was the responsibility of a section which was, in fact, older than Medmenham itself; for it began from a nucleus of veteran interpreters who had been at Bomber Command with Peter Riddell in the days of the Sylt raid. Soon after Bomber Command's 'independent' reconnaissance unit came to an end these interpreters moved to Medmenham, and from then on the section expanded rapidly. The Damage Assessment Section worked on shifts by night as well as by day: the load was an increasingly heavy one.

For the pilots, too, the 'DA' sorties were a major responsibility, and they were also, of course, especially dangerous. Some of them are among the most famous photographic flights of the war.

When Air Marshal Harris began his bomber offensive in March 1942 with the raid on the Renault factory at Billancourt, an almost equally spectacular sortie was made to check the results. The day after the raid the weather was 'impossible', but Flying Officer Victor Ricketts, with Sergeant Luckmanoff as navigator, took off from Benson in his Mosquito in heavy rain, and flew through low cloud all the way to me target. At less than 500 feet he made four runs over the factory – at the end of the second run he nearly collided with the Eiffel Tower – and came back with low-level obliques that are dicing classics.

The following summer it was Flying Officer Fray, in a Spitfire, who took the famous photographs of the Moehne

Dam the morning after it was breached. On the morning of 17 May 1943, while Fray was still over Germany, Flight Lieutenant Ronald Gillanders, who was in charge of the oncoming day shift of damage interpreters at Medmenham, answered a telephone call from the Assistant Director of Photographic Intelligence at the Air Ministry, Group Captain McNeil.

'I want you to go over to Benson right away,' he said, 'so as to be there when the aircraft lands. And phone me about the dams the moment you get the negatives.'

'What dams?' asked Gillanders.

There was a loud explosion at the other end of the telephone, and Gillanders was told to go to the Industry Section and find out. Only just through the wall from Gillander's desk was the interpreter who had been working for months on the dams in preparation for the raid.

At Benson there was tense excitement in the First Phase Section; every one from the Station Commander downwards was there, and they crowded round Gillanders as he bent over the light-table to examine the negatives. The first photographs showed nothing but flood water. Then he came to the Moehne Dam. With the crystal clear negative before him, he phoned McNeil. 'There's a gap in the centre,' he said, 'about 200 feet across. And the water is going through it *solid – solid.*'

It was in the summer of 1943 that the area bombing of German cities became so extensive that new methods had to be invented for assessing the damage. At an earlier stage the interpreters used to report on damage incidents street by street, but when the big fire raids started this method lost its point, and before long one of the interpreters developed an ingenious machine – known as 'the Damometer' – for making quick measurements of the acreage of devastation and also estimating its degree. But at the end of July, when the photographs of Hamburg came in, it seemed more a question of measuring by the square mile than by the acre. The mosaic of the Hamburg damage was so vast that it covered a whole large table.

Just at this time Field-Marshal Smuts visited Medmenham, and when he reached the Damage Assessment Section it fell to Gillanders to show him round. The Hamburg mosaic was the showpiece of the moment. Smuts came up to the table, and Gillanders pointed out the extent of the devastation, sweeping his hand right across Hamburg with a dramatic gesture. He looked up to find what impression he had made, and the sight that he saw left him utterly deflated and speechless. The tall old man with the pointed beard was shaking his head slowly from side to side, and there were tears in his eyes.

'Hamburg was a beautiful city,' he was saying, 'a beautiful city.'

• • •

While the RAF was forging ahead with area bombing, the US Eighth Air Force was beginning to operate over Germany with very different ideas. At the Casablanca Conference the Combined Chiefs of Staff had directed the Americans to go ahead with precision daylight attacks while the RAF was to continue with night bombing. But could precision daylight bombing really work? Or would the German fighters compel the Fortresses to abandon precision and work at night? One of the most cherished concepts of American air strategy was to be put to the test.

Along with the bombers of the Eighth Air Force came a squadron of photographic Lightnings; and its first commander was a First World War aviator from Texas, Major James G. Hall, whose warm friendly personality and clear-thinking drive were to make him perhaps the most popular and respected American in his field and a powerful influence for Anglo-American cooperation. Jim Hall was a well-known figure in American aviation. In the thirties he had broken flying records to publicize an anti-Prohibition group, and since then he had mixed business and flying so often that he was nicknamed 'the Flying Broker'. But when Pearl Harbour came he was 47, supposedly much too old for operational flying. With help from Elliott Roosevelt, however, he got back into the Air Corps.

When he reached England, Hall found he was expected to keep the work of his squadron 'independent', but from the start he insisted that reconnaissance photography must be coordinated all along the line, and it was largely thanks to him that early in 1943 the 13the Squadron settled at Mount Farm, the Benson satellite airfield. This move was warmly welcomed by the RAF photographic pilots, and thus began a very happy relationship.

By the end of the year two more squadrons had arrived at Mount Farm, and the American pilots were really getting the feel of the work. But they were finding, as the Mediterranean squadron had, that the performance of the Lightning was not good enough for the job. It was at this time that the new Focke-Wulf fighter, the Fw 190, was having such devastating success over Germany, and a little earlier it had looked as if even the photographic Spitfires could not meet the challenge. But fortunately a re-engined Spitfire was just ready for service. So once again the British photographic planes were flying faster and higher than anything else in the sky. Nevertheless, the threat of the German fighters was an extremely serious matter in 1943, not only to photographic reconnaissance but to the whole of the daylight bombing effort.

The Casablanca directive had given high priority to attacks on the enemy's aircraft industry, particularly the assembly factories where newly completed fighters would be destroyed. This was the wall round the orchard which had to be climbed first of all. Once over it, huge amphibious operations could be staged, and oil or any other vital target system could be attacked; but without surmounting it, little worthwhile could be accomplished.

Such was the background when I myself, because I was in charge of interpreting aircraft factories as well as aircraft, suddenly found myself deeply involved behind the scenes in the operational planning of the Eighth Air Force. The work on aircraft factories that I shared with Charles Sims was at once injected with a sense of urgent responsibility. Those scraps of evidence that we pieced together like a jig-saw puzzle – a glimpse of a fuselage outside an assembly shop, the coming and going of lorries at the loading bays, the floor areas of the workshops, the positions of the aircraft (which we found usually meant much more than mere numbers) – the meaning we found in all these things was going to be weighed against the lives of the Fortress crews.

There could be no more mistakes like a bad one I made in the very early days of my section, before I learnt that wishful thinking is about the most disastrous failing that can beset an interpreter. I had been very keen to find where a new Messerschmitt fighter, the Me 109F, was being produced, and in my enthusiasm I 'found' one (in fact it was a Ju 87) at a promising looking factory at Lemwerder near Bremen. Although my identification was questioned at once by the Air Ministry and I hurriedly retracted it, the names Me 109F and Lemwerder had been linked together in print; and the thing echoed on for months, like scandal in a gossip column, and somehow managed to creep into reports and appreciations and target material. I lived it down eventually but it was a good lesson. Very soon I learnt to question my own interpretations as a matter of course before I reported anything, and in choosing my words I developed the caution of a writer of diplomatic communiques.

It was early in 1943 that I first met Charles P. Kindleberger, who had come over to England as a member of the Enemy Objectives Unit, an American group concerned with target analysis. He was making a special study of German aircraft factories as targets for the Eighth Air Force, so he came to visit my section at Medmenham and I was at once impressed by his enthusiasm and thoroughness. After this, whenever I went to London for the Air Ministry's regular meetings on enemy aircraft production, I used to try to see Kindleberger unofficially as well.

'Kindleberger doesn't miss a thing!' I said to Sims as I dumped my brief-case down on my desk. I was just back from the meeting at the Air Ministry on 10 May. 'He thinks that Focke-Wulf Bremen is very fishy indeed.'

'What does he think is so fishy about Bremen?' asked Hazel Furney, a bouncing little brunette with a useful talent for interpreting aircraft who had recently joined my section.

'Well, as you know, we haven't had a decent cover of Bremen since the Fortress raid in April, and in our last monthly report we said "No statement" about activity. But Kindleberger wanted to know what I *sensed* was happening, so I told him that as far as we could see, on the bad photographs, the place looked more or less dead, but we couldn't actually say that in our report because the covers weren't clear enough.'

'Why wasn't he pleased?' asked Hazel.

'Because if the factory was really turning out eighty 190s a month, according to the official Air Ministry estimate, they'd have repaired it right away,' said Sims.

'And even though the raid did quite a lot of damage, production would have started again by now,' I added. 'No, actually he's very worried that the fighter production may have been moved away from Bremen *before* the raid. You know it was the biggest American attack so far, and they lost sixteen Fortresses. So just as soon as we get a good cover, he wants us to do a report on *everything* about the factory that may give a clue. And he's given me a list of the places where Focke-Wulf is supposed to have started subsidiary production, so we could start checking on those right away – if they're covered.' I glanced at my notes. 'Posen, Sorau, Cottbus, and an airfield in East Prussia called Marienburg.'

To me and my section it was exciting and encouraging that our work was obviously so badly needed; but to Charles Kindleberger, and to Colonel Richard D. Hughes (who had to take the final responsibility for recommending targets for the Eighth Air Force), it was a time of grave concern. That April attack on the Focke-Wulf factory at Bremen was the first serious effort against enemy fighter production, and now it looked as if the whole thing had misfired through faulty intelligence. All available information on the German aircraft industry would have to be reviewed afresh, in the light of the sinister possibility that dispersal eastwards was already well under way.

Spurred on by Kindleberger, Sims and I got out every back cover of Bremen over the past three years, and in June, when new photographs of the Focke-Wulf factory came in, we produced a voluninous report entitled 'Photographic Evidence relating to Focke-Wulf production'. The main thing we found was confirmation of many kinds that production of Fw 190s had stopped at the Bremen factory about six months before the American attack – and although there were fighters at the airfield right up till April they were never anywhere near the flight shed, and it looked as if they were a Luftwaffe unit based there for the defence of Bremen.

We were also able to give some startling news of dispersal, for Marienburg had been photographed once, nearly a year earlier. In the light of our growing knowledge of German methods it was clear that fighter production was in full swing even then.

Shortly after our report went out I was summoned to London to attend a special American meeting on the whole question of the dispersal of the German aircraft industry. It was an important moment, for the expanding force of German fighters was becoming a serious menace to both the Eighth Air Force and the RAF, and a new bombing directive had just been issued by the Chiefs of Staff, putting attacks on fighter factories in absolute priority.

Kindleberger had told me about Dick Hughes, 'Tooey Spaatz's right-hand, left-hand, and centre-hand,' and also about Colonel Kingman Douglass, the top American liaison officer at the Air Ministry (who in the First World War had flown reconnaissance sorties on the Western Front), but I never expected they would actually be at the meeting. But there they were were, and with them round the table were many familiar faces: Wing Commander Charles Verity, head of Air Ministry targets, with several of my other Air Ministry customers; Colonel George Jones from Eighth Air Force Intelligence; and of course Kindleberger, with Eddie Mayer, his fellow researcher on aircraft factories.

I was cross-questioned on the main findings of my report, and especially I was asked if I could confirm my statements about Marienburg. This I could do emphatically.

'Yes, it *did* have the look of a Luftwaffe base being adapted for aircraft production,' I said.

'Why are you sure?' asked Kindleberger.

'There were fourteen 190s,' I began.

'But that needn't mean fighter assembly. They might be using the field for training or as a fighter pool for the Eastern Front.'

'Yes, but one of the things that gave them away was the gun-testing range. You see, it had been fixed up with a covered firing position, which is more or less standard practice at German factory airfields, and the new aircraft shelters were of a type we see at factory airfields too.'

'Anything else?' asked Mayer.

'Yes, the way the fighters were parked. The test pilots have quite different habits from the GAF.'

Marienburg had to be photographed again as soon as possible – no doubt of that – and in future every scrap of evidence pointing towards dispersal must be checked at once by Medmenham. But the meeting decided that the question of production at Marienburg could not be finally judged on photographic evidence alone. There was not long to wait, however, and only a few weeks later I heard that salvaged Fw 190 nameplates bearing a Marienburg series of numbers had been found.

'So we can call it a factory now,' I said to Sims, 'even before we look at this new cover.' I flipped through the stack of photographs in the box file and picked out the run over Marienburg. One glance showed that a lot had happened since the previous year. There was a whacking great new hangar, and a new runway too. Nothing was camouflaged, presumably because the airfield was so far east that the Germans thought they were safe. In much excitement we set about interpreting the photographs.

Some weeks after this, late on the evening of 9 October, my telephone rang. It was Major Jack Leggett at Eighth Air Force Intelligence.

'Babs, it was Marienburg today – a terrific attack, and right on the nose! At least the strike pictures are swell, but of course we won't know the whole story till tomorrow.'

The following morning a Mosquito took off for East Prussia from Leuchars, the photographic reconnaissance base in Scotland. Squadron Leader Lenton was the pilot and Pilot Officer Haney the navigator. Their main target was Marienburg, but they also had to try for Gdynia and Danzig. Just before Danzig two Me 109s came up to intercept them, but the Mosquito escaped with ease, and went on to photograph the Focke-Wulf factory airfield. When Lenton arrived back at Leuchars he was received with joyful incredulity. He had been reported shot down and parachuting over Sylt on his way out.

When Sims and I managed to get hold of Lenton's photographs, we could hardly believe our eyes.

'That's five or six of the main buildings burnt out completely,' I exclaimed, 'and look at all the 190s smashed to pieces.'

'No mistake this time,' said Sims. 'That ought to set Mr Focke and Mr Wulf back for a bit.'

But only a week after Marienburg, the Eighth Air Force suffered such disastrous losses in attacking the Schweinfurt ball-bearing factories that American daylight operations over Germany were entirely suspended – until long-range fighter escorts could be made available. During those dark days at the end of 1943 there was one consolation, however, for those who still believed passionately in daylight precision bombing. The Marienburg photographs served as a reminder of what could be done, what *had* been done, and what would surely be done again. Meantime the list of aircraft industry targets was reviewed each week in London, against the day when precise attacks could be carried out over the heart of central Europe.

By this time my section had grown considerably and included several Americans in addition to the RAF and WAAF interpreters. Early in 1944 we moved into two spacious upstairs rooms, a former bathroom and a former bedroom, with windows that looked out southwards from one of Danesfield's grey-white towers – or ivory towers as some people would have called them. I put Sims in charge in the bedroom, and I shared the palatial ex-bathroom with two interpreters and a clerk.

We were working away as usual, noses to the stereoscope, with our pace geared to the urgent but regular tempo of keeping up with cover of the German aircraft factories, when suddenly, unexpectedly, the break-through came. It was the last week of February 1944, the famous week of brilliant frosty days, when after months of impossible weather and waiting the bombers of the Eighth and Fifteenth Air Forces, escorted by long-range fighters, let go with everything at the enemy's aircraft industry and established air supremacy over Germany for the first time.

As soon as the strike reports began to come in it was clear that something quite unprecedented was happening. And then a bewildering number of damage assessment sorties came pouring in with photographs that looked as if they had been taken during the attacks.

The factories that Sims and I had contemplated so long and late: Bernburg, Gotha, Brunswick, Fürth, Oschersleben, Regensburg, Wiener Neustadt – the assembly centres for the night fighers that threatened the RAF, as well as those for the Me 109s and Fw 190s – were hardly visible for the surging smoke that billowed up, casting strange shadows and hiding the holocaust below. And on the snow-covered airfields, thick with scattered aircraft, the black splodges made by the blast of the bombs looked as if thousands of Gargantuan bottles of ink had been hurled on the ground.

Such was the photographic record of that historic week, which for the Allies was comparable in importance to the Battle of Britain; for it meant that on D-Day fighter opposition was critically lacking in strength, and it also opened the way for the attack on oil. Inevitably it caused profound repercussions both in German production policy and in Allied plans. Before long these repercussions inevitably affected me and my section.

One day a few months later I had been lunching in the Officer's Mess when I caught sight of a familiar figure in the crowded ante-room – Peter Riddell. So he was back – and a Group Captain! After nearly three years Riddell had returned to photographic intelligence, as Senior Air Staff Officer to the RAF's first photographic reconnaissance Group at Benson. I had not seen Peter Riddell for ages, and I did not know whether he was aware that the one-woman section which he had initiated long ago at Wembley was now twelve times its original size, and that the great attacks on the German aircraft industry had been based on our reports. But he evidently did, and he greeted me with warm congratulations. Then he added cheerfully: 'But of course aircraft factory interpretations soon won't be needed any more.' I felt as if he had taken up a knife and stuck it straight into me. Surely the German aircraft industry would still have to be attacked? But perhaps Peter Riddell was right. Greatly disturbed, I went back to my section and tried to concentrate on the notes I was preparing for a talk on aircraft interpretation at the RAF Staff College.

I need not have worried, for Peter Riddell's sweeping prophecy was only partly true. Although after the spring of 1944 most of the Germans' big aircraft production centres were in such ruins that they were hardly worth attacking, yet the new jet fighters, the Me 262 and the Me 163, were already appearing in combat, to the incredulous dismay of Allied aircrews, and plans had to be made to attack jet production. So once again enemy fighter factories were high on the target priority list, which meant a new and urgent demand for our interpretations.

But this time it was different. This time Speer was in charge of the dispersal programme – determined to make aircraft production invulnerable. So in the summer of 1944, when once again I and my team set to work to hunt down dispersed aircraft factories, it was a search far and wide throughout Germany, following up reports and scraps of news to the most unimaginable hiding places: to lunatic asylums and chocolate factories, to vast fantastic underground workshops, to firebreaks in pine forests, and tunnels on autobahns. The search had a feeling of unreality about it, for one's usual standards of what was possible or impossible had to go by the board; the only thing was to go ahead and report honestly the strange facts that the camera had recorded.

On our photographs we followed the new dispersal up the valleys of the Bavarian Alps, to little villages in Silesia, to the Baltic coast, and the Polish border. In 1943 the Germans had made a habit of plastering camouflage paint over their dispersal factories, which was a great help to us, because we could then see at a glance which plants were being used for war production. But the Speer regime evidently realized that when you convert buildings from other uses the most effective camouflage is no camouflage at all. As they became more subtle in their methods we had to become more subtle too, and we watched for the most tenuous clues: for the smallest new extensions, for the slightest increase in road and rail traffic, for the special look that comes to a factory when it is busy, just as in everyday life a room looks lived in or a house looks inhabited. At the airfields where assembly was rumoured we watched for 'track activity', the accumulation of faint lines that tells an interpreter where feet or wheels have been passing over the field again and again – faint pale lines which are actually caused by the reflection of light from the myriad flattened blades of grass. And the fading of that tracery of lines at an airfield, when the grass has resumed its upward growth, means that feet and wheels have been absent. It was like the children's Grandmother's Steps, where Grandmother tries to look round so unexpectedly that she catches you actually moving. Often we could not say more than 'possibly' or 'probably', but when we *could* establish definitely that a factory was working on jet aircraft it was promptly blotted out by the bombers, like the little Bavarian shoe factory at Wasserburg, where we found some Me 262 wings lying about. That little factory was completely destroyed, but the manager was not killed, and when after VE-Day the Allied ground-check team arrived to inspect and measure the damage, his one question was 'How did you know?'

•   •   •

One day in August 1944 I went down to the print library at Medmenham to see whether there was any cover of a little place called Kahla in the Thuringian hills near Jena, as the Air Ministry had several reports of a large new jet-fighter factory there 'partly underground'. I found the map sheet I wanted, and the cover trace which showed all the areas that had been photographed. Good, there was cover of Kahla, but unfortunately not a new one – nothing since last December. However, something might have already started by then. So I collected the sortie boxes and took them upstairs to my section.

Under my stereoscope I searched the valleys with their neat little strips of fields, and the rolling hills covered with dense pinewoods, but the virgin countryside had not been touched. There was not a sign of anything but farming. No new roads or branch railways or spoil heaps. I went back over it again, and searched with special care along the fringes of the woods – that was the sort of place where a tunnel entrance might hardly show. Some months earlier I had visited a British underground factory, so I knew what to look for. But there was nothing. Still, that was six months ago. We'd have to have new cover to make sure.

Just a week later I was delighted to see on the board that Kahla had been photographed, and hurried to check whether anything had happened. A disappointment was in store: the cameras had covered Kahla all right, but just where I wanted to look there were thick patches of cloud, so I couldn't see a thing. This often happened, of course, and you just had to wait until the 'job' was photographed again. Sometimes it was a long wait, but this time good new pictures of Kahla came in only three days later. As I fastened my eyes on them, amazed at what I saw, I was glad that I should be able to share the news with someone at the Air Ministry who would really appreciate it. For since the new German dispersal began I had discovered a kindred spirit in Walt Rostow, an American economist who had come over to work on target analysis with Kindleberger and had joined the Air Ministry section concerned with German aircraft industry in the summer of 1943.

When I had gazed at Kahla for long enough, I reached

for the telephone and asked for extension 8720 at 'Monck Street', the Air Ministry's underground offices.

'Captain Rostow? I've got the new Kahla pictures, and there is an underground factory a few miles west of the town. There's a tremendous lot going on; they're tunnelling in at least two places into a long steep spur of hill covered with pinewoods, and there are several hutted camps, and a branch railway line is nearly finished.'

Kahla was only a beginning, and as report after report proved to be founded on fact it became clear that the German underground programme was in deadly earnest.

We found that an underground factory at Langenstein in the Harz mountains was one of the furthest advanced, and at Walt Rostow's instigation a model was made to help the planner to try to figure out how to attack these new targets – if they had to be attacked. Shortly after this a new section was started at Medmenham entirely devoted to underground factories, and the gigantic German burrowings kept a large team of interpreters busy until the end of the war.

But there was still one more report for my section to issue on a German underground factory. By March 1945 the long narrow mountain at Kahla had been ravaged on the grand scale, and along the summit of the ridge, high above the tunnel entrances, a strip had been shorn of trees and levelled, and a wide concrete runway laid down; while between the runway and the tunnel entrances below there was a conveyor something like a funicular railway. Here, in this fantastic Wellsian setting, we saw for the first time jet fighters that had been assembled underground.

I marvelled over the photographs with Sims and with Ursula Kay, my chief aircraft interpreter. There at the top of the conveyor were two smallish planes, and a third was down below outside a building near the tunnel entrances. The prints were not very sharp but there was no mistaking that long nose, and that high tail, and that swept-back wing. They were Me 262s.

'I'd rather not be one of the Kahla test pilots,' chuckled Sims. 'Must feel like taking off from an aircraft carrier that's got beached!'

The question whether the underground factories really were invulnerable never had to be put to the test, for jet production underground had barely started when VE-Day came. But we know now what we might have been up against, even if we discount Goering's wild claim that Kahla alone had a production capacity of more than a thousand Me 262s a month.

And during those last six months of the war in Europe, while the underground dispersal was going ahead at frantic speed, the Germans were developing yet another technique for trying to make their jet production immune from bombing. It was a most imaginative and clever dispersal of final assembly, and Ursula and I kept running it right up till a few weeks before VE-Day.

'We'll have to think of a name for these new assembly places,' I said to Ursula. 'We can't possibly call them factories; and we don't want people to think they're just ordinary airfield dispersal areas.'

'What about "Leipheim Dispersal Units"?' said Ursula. 'The first one we found was near Leipheim airfield.'

'Yes – good idea. Now let's see where we've found them: Leipheim, Neuburg, Obertraubling, and Schwäbisch Hall. All four of the main jet assembly airfields in Bavaria.'

I adjusted under my stereoscope the latest photographs of the Bubesheimer Wald, the dark plantation of pine trees that reaches southwards from Leipheim airfield beyond the broad sweep of the Stuttgart–Munich autobahn. At a quick glance you would never know that anything was going on, but there it was. For nearly half a mile two stretches of the straight grassy avenues which served as firebreaks had been screened from our view by camouflage netting fixed horizontally between the tree-trunks on either side, at a level just high enough to clear a couple of very long narrow buildings. With my stereoscope I could see the outlines of these buildings faintly through the netting, and then I could measure them with my Leitz magnifier. Their width was just wider than the wingspan of an Me 262.

'What a bit of luck that the pictures were taken in the middle of the day,' I said, 'so we can really see down into the firebreak. On the other covers it's in such deep shadow.'

I followed the track from the woods back to the autobahn, and gazed at the blurred image of an Me 262 which was being towed into position for take-off because the aeroplane was actually in movement when the photographs were taken, so it was in a slightly different position on each of the two prints of the stereo pair I was examining. The Germans were still turning out jet fighters, even though Montgomery was at Lüneburg.

We issued our report on the 'Leipheim Units' on 26 April 1945, and Walt Rostow just had time to read it before he went home to America. Then it was VE-Day and time to clear up and think ahead. I had heard that I was wanted to interpret Japanese aircraft and industry in the Pacific theatre, and would soon be posted to Washington. As I turned out my files I came on a couple of verses I had scribbled in pencil. 'Yes,' I thought, 'I might as well keep those. It was a wonderful time.'

> Between the pines at Leipheim
> The sunlight can be glimpsed,
> It's gentian time at Jenbach,
> There's edelweiss at Imst;
> The roses bloom at Kreising,
> The Wismar sea is green,
> At Oberpfaffenhofen
> Wild orchids have been seen.

Down in the Monck Street cellars
The sun can never shine;
Why should they care if lilies
Were found at Langestein?
But when at Wiener Neustadt
The grass begins to grow,
It makes a splendid reason
To ring 8–7–2–0.

•   •   •

The Allied bombing offensive against oil, which consummated the dearest ambitions of the believers in strategic precision attack, was fought to its finish during the last year of the war; but the battle could never have been waged successfully unless photographic intelligence had been watching the enemy's oil industry ever since 1940, and had been building up over the years a unique system for analysing and assessing it.

At first, when only the western edge of Germany had been photographed, the work of the interpreters was centred on the plants that extracted oil from the hard coal of the Ruhr; but soon, as the Spitfires reached out further afield, Medmenham began to confirm that the Germans were producing oil from brown coal, and were planning to develop this technique on a portentous scale.

Squadron Leader Hamshaw Thomas, by then in charge of industry interpretation, was fascinated by the Germans' brilliant exploitation of their chemical skills, and he determined to find out the capacity of the new plants. For a start he visited the few synthetic oil plants in Britain, and talked long and searchingly with the experts. Then in the summer of 1941 Leuna, near Merseburg, was photographed for the first time, and he first set eyes on the gigantic synthetic oil plant that had been constructed alongside the existing chemical works.

The straight roads that marked off the whole area into

rectangles were followed by narrower lines – the massive pipes along which the oil flowed as it progressed from stage to stage. These helped him to trace the sequence of the processes, and to deduce which equipment must be for brown coal tar, which for crude oil, and which for the final product. Next he measured up all the storage tanks, but data on the tanks alone could not give a reliable indication of the plant's capacity. All the different installations had to be analysed: the gas producers, the sulphur-removal units, the compressor houses; and finally the enormous hydrogenation stalls, in which the critical process took place at a pressure of 10,000 lb to the square inch.

When he had accumulated all this information he consulted again with the British experts, and together they were able to assess the photographic evidence in the light of known standards. Thus gradually a reliable system was evolved for estimating the maximum productive capacity of a synthetic oil plant from the interpretation of its various units.

By the beginning of 1942 Medmenham's concise estimates of production capacity were causing a revolution in intelligence on enemy oil, but the picture was still far from complete. There had been reports of a new synthetic oil plant in Czechoslovakia, but its exact location and potential output were not known. Then a clue came up. Certain German technical journals which had been smuggled to England contained advertisements for men with oil experience to work at a place called Brüx in the Sudetenland.

By this time it was possible to try for cover of such distant targets, for the Mosquitos had come into operation; so on the strength of the advertisements it was decided to 'lay on' Brüx. Early in May 1942, when successful cover was obtained, Flight Lieutenant Peter Kent, a young oil geologist who had just been put in charge of interpreting the oil plants, could hardly believe his eyes. No wonder they were advertising for personnel to go to Brüx. They would need a small army. A vast industrial complex was under construction on a site a mile and a half square. For days and weeks he interpreted and measured, calculated and discussed. At length he came up with the finding that the oil plant when complete would have a capacity of 750,000 tons a year. It was going to be a second Leuna.

From his meticulous study of Brüx Kent was able to estimate what percentage of the planned capacity was actually in use; and after this, as gradually the whole of the German synthetic oil system was photographed, he became more and more experienced at judging the actual extent of a plant's activity, by correlating the evidence he found at each stage of the process. The detailed knowledge he thus accumulated also meant that he was able to locate the most vulnerable aiming points. Soon the volume of the work on oil industry had increased so much that Kent had six interpreters helping him, including two Americans. And it was the special experience acquired by Kent and his team that made possible the purposeful planning of the offensive against oil which began in May 1944.

The score of the greatest bombing offensive against a single industry was chalked up every day on the 'oil scoreboard' which covered a whole wall beside the interpreters. On the left were the names of the thirty-five most important plants, starting with Leuna, Brüx, Pölitz, Gelsenkirchen; and at a glance you could see the comparative figures for the maximum and actual production of each. The dates of the last attack and the last cover of each were also marked up, and the date when the next cover was wanted. This last entry was a very significant one, for on it depended the timing of the next attack. Kent and his assistants could estimate how long repairs were likely to take after each raid, so the idea was to re-check by photographic cover after an appropriate interval, and stage the next attack at the moment when repairs had been made and production had just begun.

The 'oil scoreboard' was a Medmenham showpiece, and Douglas Kendall used to explain it with pride to visiting VIPs. Even when feeling was running quite high in planning and intelligence circles as to whether oil was in fact the optimum target of all time, or whether it was merely 'one of these panaceas', there was no doubt that it was an excellent strategic target-system to be watched by photographic intelligence. Not a 'quicksilver' target like the aircraft industry, that could be dispersed underground or in pine forests, it was tied to its monumental installations. This meant that in an interpreter like Peter Kent, who knew from years of experience just what he was doing, could guide the combined effort of the American and British Air Forces to the precise points where it would have the most shattering effect.

• • •

One cloudy morning in 1944 the intelligence officers at the Eighth Air Force headquarters looked eagerly at the weather forecast for the following day. It was the moment to start making definite plans for the next day's operations.

'Good bombardment weather for Leuna coming up,' said Jack Leggett as he handed the forecast to Flight Lieutenant Ivor Boggiss, liaison officer from Medmenham, 'but we haven't had cover for weeks now. We must have a mission laid on this morning.'

Messages flew over the telephone to the effect that 'the General was wild for lack of PI', and within a few hours an aircraft took off from Mount Farm. At the controls was Captain Robert Dixon, an experienced American pilot who had several times previously succeeded in photographing Leuna – at this time one of the most heavily defended targets in all Germany, with more flak ringed round it than the city of Berlin. He made a rendezvous with his fighter escort and set course for Leuna.

That afternoon Jack Leggett started making ready for the four o'clock operations conference, and first he checked again with the Met Office. Yes, the forecast of good weather for Leuna could be confirmed. Next he phoned Reconnaissance Operations and was shocked to hear that Captain Dixon's plane had not returned, and was long overdue, presumably lost.

'Better see if we can't get Peter Kent's section to say anything more from earlier covers,' suggested Boggiss.

But the interpreters were adamant. They went over the most recent photographs again, but rang back just before four o'clock to say they couldn't possibly estimate without new cover whether Leuna was actually operational again. Leggett explained all this at the operations meeting, and a final decision was postponed till nine that evening. The conference was just breaking up when the headquarters' Fighter Controller came in and asked Leggett if he could have a word with him about something urgent. 'It's a phone message from Fighter Command. They've passed it on from one of the bases.' For a moment Leggett could not imagine why a message from Fighter Command should concern him, but as soon as he read the first few words he knew: 'We arrived over Leuna with Dixon . . .' It was from the pilot of one of the escort planes. He read out the message eagerly. 'We were at 26,000, but found the area so covered with cloud that we could see nothing whatever of the target. Dixon told us to stay up where we were, and he was going down to 14,000.' Leggett paused a moment in horror, and then went on: 'He gradually worked down into the cloud, and then we heard him again. He still could not see the target and was going down to 10,000. Then we heard Dixon's voice again. "I've been hit," he said, "but I've seen the target. Tell them I've seen the chimneys in the north-west corner smoking normally. Tell Bomber headquarters that I'm sure the plant is working again. Now I'm bailing out. . . ." That's the end of the message – yes, that's all.'

On the strength of Dixon's message, it was decided to attack Leuna, and on the following day the bombs of the Eighth Air Force rained down on the largest of the German synthetic oil plants, putting it out of action yet once more.

But the happy ending to this story came the following year. Captain Dixon, who had landed safely by parachute and had been made a prisoner of war, was in due course liberated by the Allied armies, and his gallantry was recognized by the US award of the Distinguished Service Cross.

NINE

THE BATTLE AGAINST THE V-WEAPONS

Much has already been said and written about the *Vergeltung* weapons, both from the German and from the Allied viewpoints. It ranges all the way from the preliminary propaganda about *Wunderwaffen*, and from certain equally exaggerated post-war claims for the Allied counter-measures, to official histories and authoritative first-hand accounts. There is much, however, that has never been published. Almost every account of the V-weapon battle of wits alludes to the major part played by photographic intelligence in analysing and assessing the threat, but the full extent of its role and the great variety of ways in which it helped have hitherto been kept secret.

Photographic intelligence was, I need hardly say, only one of many complementary sources of information. The agents who risked their lives in Germany and the occupied countries, the interrogators who questioned the prisoners of war, the men and women who combed through trade magazines and monitored German broadcasts, the technical experts who examined V-weapon fragments; these were only a few of the vast incongruous team that supplied the raw material of the investigation. Finally, at the top, there were the intelligence experts who weighed all the varied evidence, and upon whose judgement depended what action was likely to be taken.

The story that I have to tell is not the story of how

photographic intelligence solved the V-weapon mystery single-handed, without missing a single clue. It is, rather, a strangely paradoxical story of conspicuous successes and conspicuous failures. At certain stages it brought to the overall intelligence picture a rapid accuracy and precision, and also a wideness of vision, that simply could not have existed otherwise; while at others, all the skill and perseverance of both pilots and interpreters were completely fruitless.

●　　●　　●

On 15 May 1942, Flight Lieutenant D.W. Steventon flew in his Spitfire high above the western shores of the Baltic, on the way to cover Swinemünde after photographing Kiel. Far below and ahead lay the island of Usedom, with its long belt of woodland facing the Baltic, and separated from the mainland by the River Peene. He happened to notice that there was an airfield at the northern tip of the island, with quite a lot of new developments near by, and he switched on his cameras for a short run.

At Medmenham, the Second Phase interpreters puzzled over some strange, massive ring-like things in the woods near the airfield, and they worked out the pinpoint and noted down 'heavy constructional work', and then turned their attention to destroyers off Swinemünde. The sortie then went on to the Third Phase sections as usual, for interpretation on different specialized subjects. I remember flipping through the stack of photographs and deciding the scale was too small to make it worth while looking at the aircraft. Then something unusual caught my eye, and I stopped to take a good look at some extraordinary circular embankments. I glanced quickly at the plot to see where it was, and noticed the name Peenemünde. Then I looked at the prints again. 'No,' I thought to myself, 'those don't belong to me. I wonder what on earth they are. Somebody must know all about them, I suppose.' And then dismissed the whole thing from my mind. But when the sortie finished its rounds, no one had staked a claim for the mysterious 'rings' at Peenemünde, and the cardboard boxes full of photographs were set in place on a shelf in the print library, for future reference when required. There the matter rested, as far as Medmenham was concerned, for the next seven months.

Meantime, as we know, General Dornberger and Wernher von Braun were working day and night at their rockets, and the first successful launching of an A-4 rocket – later known as the V-2 – took place at the experimental station in the woods on 3 October 1942; while in December an early version of the flying bomb, the V-1, was launched from below a large aircraft over Peenemünde.

In that same December reports of 'secret weapon trials' in this area began reaching London, and began to cause concern. The fact that the Germans were developing long-range weapons was already known to British intelligence, for a communication on plans for new weapons, including rockets, had reached London via Oslo as early as the autumn of 1939. But like those first photographs of Peenemünde that Steventon took by chance in 1942, the 'Oslo Report' had been filed away – for future reference when required.

*　　*　　*

By the beginning of 1943 there was a large and thriving section of Army interpreters at Medmenham which ministered to the needs of the War Office in matters of photographic intelligence. In February Major Norman Falcon, the officer in charge of this section, was warned by the War Office that the enemy was planning to operate 'some form of long-range projectors, capable of firing on this country from the French coast'. If this were really true, it meant a weapon of a new order. So photographic evidence relating to it might well be something very unusual. Peenemünde! What about that 'heavy constructional work' which had meant nothing to anyone the year before? Soon a further briefing came from the War Office, where it had been calculated that a rocket capable of reaching London from the French coast would have to be launched from a sharply inclined projector about a hundred yards long.

Falcon's interpreters, with several new covers of Peenemünde to work on, prepared a detailed statement. They reported a huge elliptical embankment and three circular earth banks 'not unlike empty reservoirs'. These were facts that could not be denied, but they did not in the least tally with the hypothesis of a projector a hundred yards long. Nothing seemed to tally with anything.

Such was the embryonic stage of British intelligence on 'secret weapons' when, early in April 1943, the evidence was presented to the Chiefs of Staff. But it was convincing enough to bring about the appointment of an investigator-in-chief: Mr Duncan Sandys, then Joint Parliamentary Secretary to the Ministry of Supply. The Chiefs of Staff, and the Prime Minister himself, were taking the 'secret weapon' threat seriously enough to be determined to find out just how serious it was.

Repercussions of Mr Sandys's appointment were felt immediately. The Air Ministry at once instructed Group Captain Peter Stewart (the Station Commander at Medmenham) to institute a secret weapon investigation on the highest priority. Wing Commander Hamshaw Thomas, who by this time was directing all Third Phase work, was put in charge, while an interpreter named Flight Lieutenant André Kenny and three others were assigned to search for clues of experimental work and production, especially at Peenemünde. At the same time Norman Falcon and two of his Army interpreters were to concentrate on the military side of the investigation, which meant primarily watching potential launching areas on the French Coast. Meantime, a special flying programme was laid – shared by Benson and the Americans at Mount Farm – to ensure that every square mile of the French Coast area from Cherbourg to the Belgian frontier had been photographed since the beginning of the year.

So the photographic search for secret weapons began in earnest in April 1943. No one really quite knew what they were looking for, although the Air Ministry did suggest that the interpreters should be on the look-out for three things: a long-range gun, a remotely controlled rocket aircraft, and 'some sort of tube located in a disused mine out of which a rocket could be squirted.'

On 29 April, André Kenny set off for the Ministry of Supply to report what had so far been found at Peenemünde. With Mr Sandys were his scientific advisers, two of whom had recently spent a whole day at Medmenham. Kenny spread out plans of the whole area, so that Mr Sandys could see the lie of the land, and showed him that all the main installations were at the northern end of the island of Usedom. He drew attention to the big power station at Kolpin, near the village of Peenemünde, with power lines radiating throughout the experimental station, and he explained the likely functions of the huge new workshops among the trees. There must obviously be plans for large-scale production of some kind. Then he pointed out the airfield further north, with its neat row of hangars, and beyond it some reclamation work indicating that the landing area was going to be extended. Then all eyes returned to the focal point of interest, the monumental 'earthworks' in the woods, and Kenny produced enlargements and more plans. He explained how he had come to the conclusion that the structures within some of the earthworks might well be test stands for launching missiles.

This was the first time that Mr Sandys had come into

touch with a photographic interpreter, and he was much surprised and impressed by the amount of detailed information the photography could yield. Before the meeting broke up he was firmly convinced that the whole Peenemünde site was an experimental station and that its circular and elliptical earthworks were probably for testing rockets.

On 9 May 1943 Mr Sandys visited Medmenham, where he first talked with the Army interpreters and with Kenny in the Industry Section. Then he came on to the Aircraft Section, as at this stage he was concerning himself with the search for a 'remotely controlled pilotless aircraft' as well as with rockets proper. He questioned me as to whether I had seen any aircraft at Peenemünde which I could not identify, but at this point there was nothing helpful I could say. None of the existing covers was sharp enough or of large enough scale to give the sort of information that was needed. However, from then on I knew that the airfield had to be carefully watched.

Four times in June Peenemünde was photographed. The first cover, taken on 2 June, was a good clear one, and Kenny could report quite a lot of new detail, including a 'thick vertical column about 40 feet high' on a fan-shaped stretch of open foreshore. And then on 23 June Flight Sergeant E.P.H. Peek came back with photographs that were exceptionally good. Flying in his Mosquito high over the experimental station he had been completely unaware how much was going on down below in the brilliant June sunshine, but back at Medmenham there was plenty for Hamshaw Thomas and Kenny to feast their eyes on. Two rockets – actual rockets – had been photographed, lying horizontally on road vehicles within the confines of the elliptical earthwork, and even today, after fourteen years, the superbly clear photograph makes it easy to imagine the stab of elation Kenny must have felt when he saw them.

The setting was clear in every detail too. Above the

rockets towered a structure resembling a massive observation tower, and the steep encircling slope of the earthwork might have been some sinister Germanic stadium. Beyond the great oval were the woods, and seawards, at the end of an approach road, there was the fan-shaped stretch of foreshore.

Kenny's cautiously worded report described 'torpedo-like objects thirty-eight feet long', but by the time the news had been rushed to the Prime Minister they had been definitely labelled as rockets. And within the next few days Mr Churchill directed that photographic intelligence should be enabled by every possible means to make a maximum contribution to the secret weapon investigation.

It was at this point in June 1943, that I myself was first able to say something positive about the experimental work at Peenemünde, for on the same sortie that showed those first rockets there were several runs over the airfield. My brief was to watch for 'anything queer', and the four little tailless aeroplanes that I found taking the air on 23 June looked queer enough to satisfy anybody. This was the first time I was able to analyse and measure the Messerschmitt liquid-rocket fighter, the Me 163 (which we provisionally named 'Peenemünde 30'), but it was not the first time it had been photographed at Peenemünde, as I found out within a few hours by turning up all the previous covers.

The process of going back over earlier photographs was something that was happening the entire time in the V-weapon investigation. For the sequence of photographic flights and of interpretation finds did not run smoothly parallel to the sequence of what was actually happening on the German ground. That is not the way that photographic intelligence works. Each new find was likely to throw new light on earlier photographs which had meant nothing when they were first examined. So quite apart from the normal time-lag between the date of actual photography and the date of the interpreter's report, 'first photographed' and 'first seen' often did not refer to the same cover at all.

So it was in the case of my tailless aircraft. Peenemünde airfield had been photographed eleven times before 23 June, but almost all the covers were of small scale and poor quality and I had tried in vain to find anything useful to say about those woolly-looking photographs. It had been like peering through an overlay of tracing paper – you could see blurred shapes but you couldn't possibly even hint what they were. But now that I had actually seen the tailless aircraft, and knew which buildings they frequented. I could go back to those earlier 'bits of blotting paper' and pick out pale blurred little shapes which almost certainly represented the same strange flying machines.

The photographs taken on 23 June also showed the first 'jet marks' I had ever recognized – single, dark, fan-shaped marks, from which dark streaks led out across the airfield – and in this case also I was able to go back and identify earlier streaks.

Duncan Sandys had already reported to the War Cabinet that the development of jet-propelled aircraft was probably proceeding side by side with the work on rockets and 'airborne rocket torpedoes'. The photographs of the 'Peenemünde 30' definitely confirmed this – although we now know, of course, that it did not have any direct bearing on the secrets of the V-1 and the V-2.

●   ●   ●

Meanwhile the photographs of northern France were providing ominous evidence. Early in July a ground report had reached London linking secret weapon activity with a village named Watten near Calais. Two months earlier the Army interpreters had reported on a clearing in the woods near Watten, but the spot had not been photographed since. This was quickly remedied, and the new cover showed that a great deal had happened in the interval. Work was well ahead on what was clearly going to be some gigantic concrete structure. Suspicious looking preliminaries were also going ahead at two other places in the rocket range area, and all three sites were rail-served from main lines – a fact to which many of the British rocket experts attached great importance. For by this time they were talking of 40-ton or 45-ton rockets, and missiles of this weight would have to be brought to their launching sites by rail. These theories, however, were by no means universally accepted. Lord Cherwell, in particular, could not bring himself to believe that a 40-ton rocket was a feasible proposition. He felt that a pilotless aircraft – described in one of the ground reports as 'an air mine with wings' – was much more likely to be an immediate danger.

Both in London and at Medmenham it was a time of frustrating confusion in the secret weapon investigation, which by now had been given the code-name *Bodyline* – a time of groping in the dark, of trying to lay foundations in a swamp. It was as though the parts of two or three jig-saw puzzles had been jumbled together, and it was sorely tempting to try to find only one answer – only one weapon. It seemed a triumph when two or three bits of puzzle fitted together and could be identified as 'Rocket'; and it was all too easy to ignore the bits which did not fit in with these.

In spite of the conflicting views about rockets, however, Duncan Sandys was convinced that the secret weapon threat was a grave one. Soon the decision was made to attack Peenemünde. On the night of 17 August 1943, when Bomber Command made their famous raid, forty aircraft were lost, but considerable destruction was caused. We know now that it seriously delayed the whole V-2 programme, though estimates of just how long a delay it caused vary from four weeks to six months.

Then ten days later, on 27 August, the US Eighth Air Force attacked Watten. The attack on the 'launching shelter' for V-2s, as General Dornberger calls it, could not possibly have been better timed, for a huge mass of concrete was in process of hardening when the bombs came down, and within a day or two a chaotic jumble of steel, props, and planking was utterly rigid and immovable. Sir Malcolm McAlpine, the eminent engineer, who was asked to comment on the damage assessment photographs, said, 'It would be easier to start over again.' According to General Dornberger, the German engineer in charge shared his view.

•   •   •

During the spring and summer of 1943 there had been two main currents of V-weapon interpretation at Medmenham: the work of Kenny and his helpers, concerned chiefly with Peenemünde itself; and that of the Army interpreters under Norman Falcon and his second-in-command Captain Neil Simon, who struggled to make sense out of the early developments at Watten and the other 'heavy sites' in France. In September there was a readjustment of responsibility. Douglas Kendall was given direction of the whole investigation by Hamshaw Thomas, and Norman Falcon agreed that the Army interpreters involved should expand the scope of their work to include all types of possible V-weapon activity.

Kendall was by this time a Wing Commander and in charge of Second Phase, the Model Making Section, the topographical reporting, and much else. In the daytime he never had a moment for interpretation, but when evening came he always gravitated toward the Army Section, eager to see any new *Bodyline* finds: any new 'unidentified activity', any trees being felled in the woods of the Pas-de-Calais, any dumps of building materials in the little valleys of the Cherbourg peninsula – and especially any signs of new railway spurs.

Almost every day there were sinister new activities to be examined. Near Mimoyecques, not far from Cap Gris Nez, a new railway spur was being tunnelled right through a hill, and was surmounted by three phoney 'haystacks' which might very well hide nearly vertical shafts. This might tie in with those peculiar rumours of rockets that were going to be squirted up from underground, but what more could one say? At Sottevast and Martinvast, near Cherbourg, there were burrowings and scrapings and new railway spurs; and at Siracourt, Lottinghem, and Wizernes, between Calais and the Somme, the same sort of goings-on; but all at such an early stage that they might develop into almost anything.

In retrospect it is not surprising that the heavy sites were so hard to understand, for they were not, in fact, a related system of launching sites for a single type of weapon. Four of them were intended as 'launching shelters' for V-2s; two as mammoth launching sites for V-1s; and Mimoyecques was to have housed a multi-barrelled long-range gun which never materialized at all.

At the Ministry of Supply, on 21 October, Duncan Sandys decided the rocket danger was so grave that the whole suspect area must be re-photographed. For the third time a flying programme involving a hundred separate sorties was laid on: a hundred separate sorties, each consisting of hundreds of photographs, every one of which had to be scanned with care. During the first week of November the full effects of this hit Medmenham. Each day the box-files stacked up in towering mountains around the Army interpreter whose job it was to 'watch France': Captain Robet Rowell. Doggedly he ploughed through the piles of prints, searching for railway spurs and for scratchings and burrowings that had not been there before. It was not yet a hunt for actual rockets, of course, but it was very definitely a hunt for rocket launching sites – for *rail-served* rocket launching sites.

Into this rocket-conscious atmosphere there came suddenly, on 4 November 1943, a major new discovery, which at first did not seem to fit in anywhere. On the contrary, it merely seemed to add a new complication. A few days earlier a report had reached London from an agent in France, telling that the construction firm he had worked for was engaged on building eight 'sites' in the Pas-de-Calais, not far from Abbeville. He could not understand what they were for, though he strongly suspected they had to do with secret weapons; but he could describe exactly where they were. On 3 November the eight places in question were photographed.

When the specially flown sorties arrived at Medmenham Neil Simon offered to lend a hand, as Rowell was already swamped with work. Later they puzzled together over what they had found – in some disappointment. There was something 'starting' all right at each of the eight pinpoints, and it was evidently the same 'something' in each case. But there was no railway anywhere near, let alone new rail spurs leading to the sites.

Late that evening, when Douglas Kendall got back from a day's meetings in London, he made straight for the Army Section. With Simon and Rowell he looked quickly at each of the eight sites – each one partly in a wood, and each apparently to have a set of nine standard buildings, some of them strangely shaped. Then he settled down to gaze at the site which was furthest advanced. It was near Yvrench, in a wood called Bois Carré. Three of the buildings were unlike anything he had ever seen in his life. Except – yes – they were like something. They took his mind back to winter sports before the war, for they reminded him of skis.

'Skis,' he thought aloud. 'That's what they look like – skis.' Two of them seemed to be identical, and the third was shorter; and each, in plan view, had one gently curving end. They were like a giant's skis laid down on their sides.

Through the early hours of the morning the *Bodyline* interpreters measured and checked, compared and discussed. Each clearing and each pit, each dump of building materials, each semi-complete building, each road and path, was analysed from the viewpoint of the overriding question of the day: 'What is the connection with rockets?' But at the end of it all the answer was inconclusive. These new sites might be for launching projectiles of some sort, but they bore no relation to anything else that had been found so far.

When the report on these eight curious sites reached its recipients in London, it added no fuel to the flames of controversy that were raging more fiercely than ever in *Bodyline* circles. These new sites, whatever they might be intended for, were apparently not for rockets. The two schools of thought about secret weapons that had grown up during the past six months were by now coming into conflict. Duncan Sandys himself led the group which believed that the long-range rocket was the only weapon that really mattered; while the others, including Lord Cherwell, stuck to their guns in differing with him. There were one or two scientists in this group who even maintained that Peenemünde was a gigantic hoax and that the rockets photographed there were dummies. Things reached such an impasse that the Prime Minister himself intervened. He appointed Sir Stafford Cripps, then Minister of Aircraft Production, to examine the facts and decide whether the German secret weapons really existed at all, and if so what was the nature and extent of the threat. A meeting was called for the morning of 8 November 1943, at which the primary evidence was to be examined.

In the conference room at the Cabinet Offices Sir Stafford Cripps sat at the head of the great U-shaped table, and on either side of him was a splendid array of Generals and Admirals and Air Marshals, as well as Duncan Sandys representing the Prime Minister and a train of distinguished scientific advisers. At one side of the table, in the bottom three places, were Douglas Kendall, Neil Simon, and André Kenny.

The first evidence to be presented consisted of reports from agents and other secret sources. It was, on the whole, vague and lacking in detail. Some of it referred to rockets, but there were also allusions to pilotless aircraft. Then came an analysis of German propaganda, which tended to confirm the existence of German secret weapons, but only in an indirect manner.

It is a startling thought that those first witnesses gave the sum total of primary evidence from sources other than aerial photographs. If no such thing as photographic reconnaissance had existed, and if the interpreters had not been waiting at the bottom of the table, those vague ground reports and the analysis of propaganda would have been the only basis for Sir Stafford Cripps's judgement.

The opening stages of the meeting can, indeed, be compared to the opening stages of the meeting which once took place in ancient Babylon, in the days of Belshazzar the king:

> Then came in all the king's wise men: but they could not read the writing, nor make known to the king the interpretation thereof.

As it was, however, the better part of the meeting at the Cabinet Offices was given over to discussing the photographic evidence.

First of all Kenny spoke about Peenemünde; the rockets that had been seen there and the effects of the RAF attack. Then the questioning switched to Watten and the other heavy sites in France. Kendall described what had been found at each. At last there was a pause, but Sir Stafford had one more question.

'Apart from the heavy sites, have you any other information to suggest secret weapon activity in northern France?'

'Yes,' replied Kendall, 'we have.'

The attention of the meeting which had been wilting somewhat as one heavy site after another was discussed, was suddenly electrified. There was breathless silence as Sir Stafford asked, 'What have you found?'

'A new sort of installation, almost certainly a launching site of some kind. A whole system of them is being built in the Pas-de-Calais.'

'How many are there?'

'Up to midnight last night we'd found nineteen.'

'Nineteen! 'Nineteen!' echoed round the table.

'Probably more have been found by now,' went on Kendall. 'We've only had time to search part of the *Bodyline* area.'

'Why do you think they have anything to do with secret weapons?' asked Sir Stafford.

'They are not like any known military installation,' explained Kendall, 'and they were all started at once. And each of them is apparently going to have a firing-point aimed at London.'

Sir Stafford immediately decided to adjourn the meeting for two days, so as to give the interpreters a day and two nights to complete their search for the new sites, and to prepare a detailed analysis.

By the time the meeting reassembled on 10 November, a total of twenty-six 'ski sites' had been found. But no clues had yet been discovered to show what sort of missile they were meant for. In the report which Sir Stafford Cripps submitted to the War Cabinet a few days later, however, he judged that pilotless aircraft were a more immediately danger than long-range rockets. He also advised that photographic cover of Peenemünde and of the danger area in France should be kept up.

The 'Stafford Cripps meeting' helped to cause a general shake-up in *Bodyline*. Duncan Sandys's special investigation came to an end, though he continued to advise on rockets; and on 18 November the responsibility both for intelligence and for planning counter-measures passed to the Air Staff.

A fortnight after the meeting no less than ninety-five ski sites had been identified. The vast majority were in the Pas-de-Calais, with their firing points on the 'London line', but there were also groups in the Cherbourg peninsula aiming at Plymouth and Bristol.

'We've *got* to find out what they're for and how they work,' said Kendall to Falcon one evening, as they returned to the Army Section after dinner in the Mess. 'I don't feel we've really proved yet that they're not for rockets.' They were joined by Robert Rowell and Neil Simon, and the four of them, surrounded by a sea of photographs, plunged once more into argument and counter-argument.

'If the "ski buildings" really are for storage, which seems the most likely thing,' began Falcon, 'the shape and size of the things to be stored in them is fairly limited.'

Kendall put the latest cover of the Bois Carré site under a stereoscope, and gazed yet again at the absurdly long flat-roofed windowless buildings. They were nearly 260 feet long, but their width was only just ten feet.

'What we've got to check,' he said, 'is the radius of curvature at the entrance, so as to make sure whether a rocket could be moved in and out.'

'I've calculated that a 38-foot rocket, like the ones at Peenemünde, could just be manoeuvred into a ski building,' said Simon, 'at least without its fins on.'

Perhaps that was why the third ski building was always shorter than the other two, thought Kendall. It might be for the smaller components of the rocket.

'So there are no grounds for ruling out rockets as far as

the actual ski buildings are concerned,' he said. 'But I think the firing-points are a different story.'

He set in position a different pair of photographs, which showed the furthest advanced of the oblong platforms, and his eyes fastened on the platform's narrow extension on which was a row of two-foot upright concrete studs – six pairs of them, twenty feet apart, like a set of buttons down the front of a double-breasted coat.

'Yes,' agreed Falcon, 'I think so too. Because if you were going to put up an apparatus for launching rockets at a steep angle, you wouldn't start by making a platform with a long row of concrete studs.'

'Those studs are just the sort of foundations you'd need,' put in Rowell, 'if you were going to set up steel posts to support something like a bridge.'

'A bridge,' repeated Kendall, 'perhaps something like an inclined bridge.'

'In other words a ramp,' remarked Falcon. 'And that wouldn't be any use at all for launching rockets, because if you launched a rocket at such a low angle it would fall to the ground almost at once.'

'But if the thing had wings to give it a lift,' argued Kendall, 'then you would *want* to launch it from a ramp and not vertically.'

'You couldn't get a missile with wings round the corners of the ski building,' Simon pointed out.

There was silence for a minute.

'What about the very small concrete building at the other end of the platform from the studs?' Rowell asked Kendall. 'Have you any ideas about that?'

Kendall laughed. 'Don't you think that's for the gentleman who presses the button?' he said. 'An interesting job, no doubt, but judging by the strength and the shape of the building I should think it might be a bit uncomfortable at times.'

They went on to discuss a square building which in every case was placed exactly in line with the firing-point.

Kendall turned up some low obliques of the Bois Carré site, which showed the square building very clearly, with its wide entrance facing towards London.

'What was the width of the door?' he asked Simon.

'Twenty-two feet across.'

'Twenty-two. Hm. So just supposing the missile had its wings put on to it in this building, its wing-span would have to be less than twenty-two feet. Right?'

'And if the wings weren't put on till the last minute,' added Falcon, 'the components could be stored in the ski buildings.'

'But why should the square building be so carefully oriented to London?' said Kendall. 'It must be something to do with setting directional control. The missile *could* have a magnetically directed automatic pilot, I suppose.'

Before the end of November Kendall had issued a report suggesting that the missile to be fired from the ski sites was a flying bomb. He also described in detail the likely firing procedure. But his seemingly over-confident interpretation was not immediately accepted by some who were still thinking in terms of rockets. On 1 December Douglas Kendall, accompanied once more by Neil Simon, was summoned to an intelligence meeting at the Cabinet Offices, to try to justify his theories and claims.

I must now go back a little, to describe the stage my own work was reaching on the sidelines of the secret weapon investigation. First I should emphasize that until November 1943 my contact with *Bodyline* consisted of two things only: my brief to watch Peenemünde airfield for 'anything queer', and my discovery and analysis of the 'Peenemünde 30' and the marks it left on the ground. I had no idea that Kenny had found rockets, I knew nothing of the 'Stafford Cripps meeting', and the name 'ski site' would have had no meaning whatever for me – if I had ever heard it.

On 13 November, however, Kendall came and asked me to search afresh at Peenemünde for an aircraft which might be pilotless. My interest in the secret weapon hunt had been flagging a bit, but Kendall's enthusiasm revived it, especially as he gave me something specific to look for: a very small aircraft, smaller than a fighter. This was the first time I had been briefed in these terms.

Something smaller than a fighter would only show up on good photographs, so I went to the library and fetched the famous set of photographs on which I had earlier found the 'Peenemünde 30s'. It was by far the best of the early covers, and, sure enough, I did find a midget aircraft on those splendid photographs. The absurd little object was not on the airfield, but sitting in a corner of a small enclosure some way behind the hangars, immediately adjoining a building which I suspected, from its design, was used for testing jet engines. Similar buildings had recently been put up at several of the German aero-engine factories. I named it 'Peenemünde 20', as its span was about 20 feet, but there was precious little I could say about it. The midget aircraft had the aggravating cotton-wool look that all light-coloured or shiny objects acquire on aerial photographs, owing to the 'light-spread' that blots out shadow and prevents detailed interpretation, and also makes things look deceptively larger than they are.

But Kendall, and also Golovine at the Air Ministry, seemed certain that the 'Peenemünde 20' was very important, and they urged me to continue my search. So during the next two weeks I got out more back covers, intent on probing into all the most unlikely corners.

It so happened that, while this search was in progress, on the morning of 28 November 1943, a Mosquito was on its way across the North Sea from Scotland to try for 'DA' cover of Berlin. It was a time of steady bad weather over central Europe, and a whole series of attempts to photograph Berlin had failed.

The pilot was Squadron Leader John Merifield, who since Alistair Taylor went missing was quietly emerging as the steadiest and most talented of the Mosquito pilots at Leuchars. It was Merifield (when war broke out he was a nineteen-year-old undergraduate at Oxford) who in March 1942 had flown the first cover of Königsberg – a landmark of great significance: for the first time the whole of northern Germany was within range.

Merifield and his navigator, Flying Officer Whalley, approached the Berlin area from the north, but when they reached the city they realized that they would not be able to take any photographs there. The cloud was solid below them. Merifield knew, however, that it was much clearer on the Baltic coast, as they had come in that way. So he turned northwards and set course for the alternative targets that had been picked for him at briefing. There were some shipping targets at Stettin and Swinemünde, a flock of airfields, a suspected radar installation at Zinnowitz on the island of Usedom, and various other odd jobs. One after another Merifield photographed them. After Zinnowitz there was still some film left, and Merifield always made a point of using up every scrap. What targets were left? The airfield at Peenemünde. That would just about do it. Flying westwards, Merifield switched on his cameras as he reached the northern tip of Usedom, and they clicked away as he crossed the airfield. Then home!

Three days later, on 1 December, while Kendall was arguing his case at the meeting in London, explaining step by step why he believed so strongly that the ski sites were for launching flying bombs, I was still combing Peenemünde for midgets. There was by this time a big accumulation of back covers, and re-examining them was an undertaking of some magnitude.

The fact that I had found the 'Peenemünde 20' near a building I thought was an engine test-house led me to cast my eyes further afield than usual, towards the no-man's land which lay between the area I was officially watching and the woods that marked the edge of the main experimental station – the domain of the Industry and Army Sections.

There were four rather fancy modern buildings set by themselves in the open here, which I was sure housed some sort of dynamometer test beds. I had made a close study of test beds, because Walt Rostow and the American target experts had wanted to know the numbers at each German factory – as evidence of potential output. I had consulted with authorities on the subject at Farnborough and the Ministry of Aircraft Production as well as one of the Rolls-Royce factories, and I did not think anyone at Medmenham would contest my right to appropriate these buildings at Peenemünde. I checked the activity near them from cover to cover, and surprisingly, I thought, I did find one crumb of evidence to link them with the 'Peenemünde 20'. On several dates there was an object resembling a midget air-frame outside one of them.

This first excursion beyond the official bounds of the airfield encouraged me to try my luck in other directions, and I decided to follow the dead straight road which led northwards along the eastern boundary of the airfield toward the Baltic shore. I passed the limits of the airfield and went on towards the extreme edge of the island. To the right lay an untouched stretch of marshy foreland, but on the left there was a great deal going on – the long-term project of land reclamation for extending the airfield. I could see the plumes of smoke from the bucket-ladder dredgers chugging away offshore, and there were several suction dredgers with their long spidery pipes straggling over the huge semi-circle of land which showed up with the hard black and white of constructional work against the settled greys of the airfield and its surroundings.

I was not in the least interested in the dredging or the

land reclamation, which anyway did not 'belong' to me. There was a separate section at Medmenham whose sole job was to watch and report on developments at airfields. So I ignored the portentous reclamation scheme, and pursued the straight road leading to the water's edge. Right at the end of the road was something I did not understand – unlike anything I had seen before.'

Charles Sims was working at the other side of the room, and I said to him: 'Do come and have a look at something here.' Sims came over and looked, but like me he was completely nonplussed by the unusual structures I had stumbled upon. I bent down again over the photographs.

'Surely,' I said to Sims, 'this is the sort of thing you would put up if you wanted to launch something out to sea, isn't it?'

Rumours of 'launching rails' for secret weapons had reached me earlier, and ever since I had been briefed about pilotless aircraft I had been on the look-out for a catapult of some kind.

I pondered over the photographs and reviewed what I had found. There were four of these strange structures. Three of them looked very much like the sort of cranes that have a box for the operator and a long movable arm. But the fourth seemed different, and it was the one that drew my attention most. It was evidently a sort of ramp banked up with earth – you could tell that from the shadow – supporting rails that inclined upwards towards the water's edge. 'I'd better check with the Industry interpreters,' was my first thought.' So I took the prints along to the Industry Section, and was told that these 'things' had been looked at long ago, and interpreted as something to do with the dredging equipment.

Back at my desk I gazed at the photographs again. 'I don't believe it,' I thought. 'I must show them to Kendall.' So I phoned his office. Kendall was in London, I was told, and might not be back till fairly late. I asked that the moment he arrived he should be told I would like to see him.

I knew there was a new cover of Peenemünde, flown on 28 November, but I had no right to claim the photographs before the various sections with higher priorities. Late in the afternoon, however, I said to Ursula Kay, 'Do try and get that new cover of Peenemünde,' and off she went to track it down.

When the door opened, I looked up expecting to see Ursula, but it was Douglas Kendall, still with his coat on, and carrying his brief-case. He looked a bit white and tired, I thought.

'I hear you want to see me, Babs,' he said.

'Yes, I do. I want you to look at something I've found at Peenemünde. Don't you think it *might* be a catapult for pilotless aircraft?'

I showed him one of the single prints, and he was so silent for a minute that I thought he must share the views of the Industry Section.

Then he said: 'That's *it*! Let's see the pair,' and he quickly set my stereoscope over the two photographs. I couldn't understand why he was immediately so certain. 'You think it *is* for launching pilotless aircraft, then?' I asked.

'I *know* it is.' He took up the photographs. 'I'll just take these along to the Army Section. You can have them back soon.'

He was gone before Ursula returned, proudly carrying a box file. Together she and I looked at the plot, and my chief anxiety was as to whether the run over Peenemünde airfield started in time to include the landing place. Fortunately it did – just. Only the first print of the run showed it, and there was no stereo pair. The quality of the photograph was poor, but even with the naked eye I could see that on the ramp was something that had not been there before. A tiny cruciform shape, set exactly on the lower end of the inclined rails – a midget aircraft actually in position for launching.

Late through that night I worked feverishly with

Kendall to trace back the history of the 'Peenemünde Airfield Site'. We found that the first experimental ramp had been built late in 1942, during the interval between the earliest two covers of the area. Kendall himself measured and analysed the ramp and then started drafting an immediate report.

But the ramp near the airfield was not the only one on the Baltic coast that was reported by Medmenham on 1 December 1943. John Merifield's sortie had brought another piece of exciting news as well. The Air Ministry had asked for photographs of the 'suspected radar installation at Zinnowitz' because they had heard that a Luftwaffe unit was plotting flying bombs launched from this location. So Claude Wavell, as the top radar interpreter, and Neil Simon and Robert Rowell in the Army Section, had been searching the wooded shoreline. And almost at the same moment that I was looking at the earlier cover, and asking myself what on earth the ramp near the airfield could be, they had found, between Zinnowitz and the village of Kempin, eight miles away down the coast of Usedom, a launching site with firing-points aiming out to sea, which also matched up with the foundations for ramps at the ski sites. It was, in fact, a Luftwaffe centre for training the personnel who were going to operate the launching sites in France.

Before daylight next morning Kendall's report on both Peenemünde and Zinnowitz was on its way to London, with the news that the nature of the most imminent cross-Channel threat was at last established beyond doubt. It was going to be a flying bomb.

•　　•　　•

Crossbow! This code-word superseded *Bodyline* once it was known for certain that the flying bomb – the V-1 – was the danger to be countered first. At this point it seemed that the V-1 attacks, when they came, might be of an appalling magnitude. The ski buildings provided storage space for twenty flying bombs at each site, and as there were nearly a hundred sites it seemed possible that the target for launchings was something like 2,000 flying bombs in each twenty-four hours.*

When was this deluge of flying bombs supposed to begin? That was the next question, and Kendall and the Army interpreters had been busy working out the answer even before it was asked. So many sites had been photographed in France that the average time needed for the early stages of construction could be calculated very accurately, and the photographs of Peenemünde and Zinnowitz helped to fill in the rest of the story. Kendall discussed the technical problems with several interpreters who were peacetime architects, and finally came out with an estimate that the minimum time for construction of a ski site was 120 days from start to finish. So the target date for the beginning of the attack might be about six weeks ahead.

The ski sites had obviously got to be bombed, and at once Medmenham embarked on the huge job of providing material for targeting. Kendall also invented a method of assessing the readiness of each site, so that attacks could be timed for the moment when construction was far advanced but not too dangerously near completion. He worked out a 'points system', allocating a hundred points to each site, and a certain number to each individual building. When new cover came in, the interpreters assessed the readiness of each building in points, and their total represented the percentage of readiness of the whole site.

But at the end of December 1943, when the Allied air forces really let fly at the ski sites – the heavy bombers of

* A hundred per twenty-four hours was the average actually launched during the main flying-bomb offensive.

the Eighth Air Force were brought in with devastating effect – every site was flattened, whether it was nearly ready or not. Soon the whole system of ski sites was a shambles. The first round of the battle against the flying bomb was an overwhelming victory for the Allies.

When the bombing of the ski sites first began, the Germans had tried frantically to repair all the damage. But as the attacks grew heavier the policy seemed to change and repair work was concentrated on the firing-point and the square building. 'So those must be the real essentials,' thought Kendall, as he saw this happening at site after site.

The elaborate storage 'skis' and certain other buildings at the sites were not essential to the actual launching, although they *would* have been essential to the really heavy bombardment that the Germans originally planned.

At the end of April 1944 – little more than a month before D-Day – Robert Rowell was examining a new cover of the Cherbourg peninsula when he suddenly gasped. Near a village called Belhamelin something peculiar had been constructed between two farm buildings. It could be – yes it must be – yes it was – a long concrete platform with pairs of studs embedded in it. Ah! The beginnings of a firing-point. And some way from it, in a field, was a heavily camouflaged square building. The two essential installations! It was a launching site of a new, much simpler variety, and the camouflage and dispersal was extremely subtle. The Germans had evidently learnt their lesson over the ski sites, and had made new plans with Allied interpreters as well as Allied bombing in mind. The new sites were horribly difficult to spot, but within a few days twelve had been identified.

These finds sounded off a new *Crossbow* alarm, and for the fourth time a special flying programme was laid on. The whole area within 150 miles of London,

Southampton, and Plymouth was to be photographed yet again. At Medmenham, Kendall put fifteen more interpreters to *Crossbow* work.

By the beginning of June sixty-eight 'modified sites' had been found, most of them oriented to the 'London line'. But one rather puzzling thing came to light. Once the concrete bases for the ramp and the square building were laid, nothing more happened. Could there be a hold-up somewhere? No. It was according to plan that the modified sites were left unfinished. The answer to this was found not in France but at the V-1 training centre at Zinnowitz. New cover showed that an additional landing site, of the modified type, were being completed there. So Kendall and Rowell were able to observe the manner in which one of these sites was made ready for use. Sections of rail six metres long were brought to the site, and there they were fitted together and erected; while prefabricated parts for the square building were also assembled on the spot.

The very day before D-Day Kendall broke this news to a *Crossbow* meeting in London. Its grave implication was, of course, that the modified sites in France, and also perhaps some of the ski sites which had seemed to be abandoned, could be made ready for use within a matter of forty-eight hours. The first warning would be the arrival of components for the ramp and the square building. It was therefore agreed that if this were seen, a signal should immediately be sent to the Air Ministry with the code-word *Diver*.

During the first few days after the Normandy landings *Crossbow* priorities counted for nothing in the reconnaissance programme. 'We'll just have to make do as best we can with chance covers of the sites,' said Kendall to Rowell, 'but we must brief all the interpreters very carefully, and tell them how vitally important it is to spot any components.'

By 11 June there were special *Crossbow* sorties again, and late that evening photographs of nine of the sites, which had not been covered since D-Day, were brought to Kendall. He took one look at them and sent off the *Diver* signal. It was in the early hours of the morning of 13 June that the first V-1 landed in Britain.

•   •   •

During the hectic weeks and months that led up to the sending of the *Diver* signal the attempt to solve the mystery of the other secret weapon – the V-2 rocket – had of necessity taken second place. But a few new clues had been found.

In March 1944 a report had reached London that the Germans were making rocket trials at a place called Blizna in the wilds of south-east Poland. Could Blizna be photographed to confirm or disprove the report? Yes, it could. Blizna was a thousand miles from Benson, right across Germany, but only six hundred from San Severo, the photographic reconnaissance base in Italy. So on 15 April a Mosquito from Italy set off for Poland, and far above the forests and marshes between the Vistula and the San photographs were taken of the clearing where the rocket launching had been reported.

Back at Medmenham, Kendall and the Army interpreters pored over the photographs – the place smelt of *Crossbow*, but there were no rockets to be seen, and none of the big earthworks as at Peenemünde. When Blizna was covered a second time, however, on 5 May, a rocket happened to be in the open. And by comparing the photographs of Blizna with those of Peenemünde it could be established that the rockets had four fins, and that the huge trailers used for moving them were of a special design. This tied up with ground reports of special road vehicles known as *Meillerwagen*.

Such scraps of evidence were very valuable, but they could do little to clarify the strongly differing views of the various authorities in London as to how the rocket worked and how it was launched. There was still no agreement, when, towards the end of July, amid the stuttering of approaching V-1s, the War Cabinet began to be seriously concerned about the possibility of imminent rocket attack. The whole investigation was once again charged with high urgency. It was a challenge to Medmenham.

Kendall decided that the only thing was to go back over all the previous covers of Peenemünde. Many of them had been interpreted at an early stage of the secret weapon investigation, at a time when the most dominant theories insisted on a huge rocket that could not be launched vertically and could be moved only by rail. Now there were a number of reports of vertical launching and the evidence of the old photographs might appear in quite a fresh light.

Kendall made his way to the long narrow room where the *Crossbow* interpreters worked, and sought out Robert Rowell. They agreed to tackle the huge job, which would mean re-examining thirty-five sorties. Evening after evening Kendall returned to the task, Stooped low over the photographs, he would often remain motionless for minutes at a time. One of the best interpreters at Medmenham once said, 'I don't look for things; I let the photographs speak to me,' and that was Kendall's approach. Gradually the old photographs began to tell a startling new story.

He re-examined the great earthworks that dominated the scene, but then his attention focused on the fan-shaped stretch of foreshore that lay to seaward. At the end of the short road from the elliptical earthwork it looked almost as bleakly bare as a parade ground. He checked it patiently from cover to cover, and then at last sat back.

'Yes, it's asphalt,' he said to Rowell. 'I've found when they started laying it. The Germans wouldn't lay all that asphalt without good reason.' He returned to his stereoscope. Then after a minute or two he handed a pair of prints to Rowell.

'This is the "column forty-feet high" which was photographed last June. Have a look and see what you make of it.'

Rowell looked, and then gave an explosive laugh.

'A column forty-feet high my foot! It's a rocket sitting on its fins!'

Kendall smiled and nodded. 'That's why they needed the asphalt. The fan-shaped foreshore must be a practice site for operational launchings. The elliptical earthwork was for the early experiments.'

He bent down once more over his stereoscope.

'So that really is the end of the theory that the launching sites have to be rail served,' he went on, looking searchingly at the stretch of asphalt. It was innocent of anything resembling a railway line. 'And the only signs of an operational launching site will be a bit of concrete or asphalt.'

'They wouldn't even have to bother with that, would they?' said Rowell. 'A bit of any main road would do just as well.'

From 8 September 1944, when the first V-2 was launched against England, throughout the months during which the 'drizzle of rockets' continued, innumerable sorties were flown to pinpoints that had been reported as launching sites, and the interpreters searched thousands upon thousands of photographs. But in only two cases – where clearings in woods were found at the suspected spots – could any suspicious signs be reported. Not one single operational launching site was found. In fact they did not exist. As General Dornberger explains in his book *V-2*, the rocket could be launched from 'a bit of planking on a forest track, or the overgrown track itself'. The only hope of spotting a V-2 launching site was if a photographic aircraft happened to pass overhead when a rocket was set upright being fuelled. Otherwise there was virtually nothing to see, for the *Meillerwagen* was easily concealed under trees. It was a one in a million chance, and even if it occurred it would not provide a target for attack, as the 'sites' were completely mobile. Nevertheless, the frustrating search had to go on.

Such impotence, such lagging far behind reports from other sources, was something quite new for photographic intelligence. The ground reports were very emphatic at this time, as one might expect. To the residents of The Hague, the thunderous roar of rockets made it only too clear that the Haagsche Bosch was the main launching area. Eventually, it was on photographs of The Hague that operational rockets were first found by the interpreters. On 29 December there were thirteen of them, 'concealed' under the trees in The Hague's main park. Evidently this was a forward storage point as well as a launching area.

During the first weeks of the new year, however, the Allied attacks on the Haagsche Bosch succeeded in driving the Germans out of it, and London had a brief respite from V-2s. But then the rockets started coming over again. Where were they coming from?

On the afternoon of 26 February 1945 Flight Lieutenant George Reynolds, one of the day shift of *Crossbow* interpreters, picked up a sortie box and opened the plot. It was new cover of The Hague, 'Jolly good quality,' thought Reynolds, as he glanced through the stack of photographs, and he felt sorry that he was just due to hand over to the next shift. 'But I'll just have time to start looking through it,' he thought. He began working through the sortie and then suddenly called across the room to Rowell: 'Robert! Quick! Come and look at this.'

The million-to-one chance had come off. There it was, clear as you like, a V-2 rocket sitting on its fins, with fuelling vehicles clustered round. So this was the new launching area: Duindigt racecourse in the north-east suburbs of The Hague. Could it be a storage area too?

But the Germans were managing to dispense with forward storage points altogether. During the following month, until the V-2 attacks ended on 27 March 1945, only an occasional rocket on a *Meillerwagen* was to be seen.

If Hitler's ideas of sticking to massive concrete 'launching shelters' had prevailed, the tale would have been very different. There would have been something to bite on. But the plain fact of the matter is that General Dornberger's almost ridiculously simple conception of how the V-2s should be launched defeated Allied photographic reconnaissance.

TEN

THE LAST STAGES IN EUROPE

A few weeks before D-Day the concept of strategic photographic reconnaissance which had finally come to be accepted as the ideal was implemented on the grand scale. It was the same simple concept that had been demonstrated in embryo in the days of the Photographic Development Unit: a flexible organization supplying all three Services, with one central control point.

Benson became the hub of a large, delicately balanced combination. There a joint committee (which was responsible directly to the Combined Chiefs of Staff) co-ordinated the priorities of the flying programme; while geared to this committee and to one another were the American 'P.R.' headquarters at High Wycombe, the squadrons at Benson and Mount Farm, and the interpretation unit at Medmenham.

There were two squadrons of Mosquitos and two of Spitfires at Benson, belonging to a newly formed British photographic reconnaissance Group under the command of Air Commodore John Boothman – winner of the Schneider Trophy in 1931. His Senior Air Staff Officer was Peter Riddell, who also shared with an American colonel named Carlton G. Ketchum in guiding the joint committee. Meantime, at the Eighth Air Force headquarters at High Wycombe, Elliott Roosevelt presided over a new US reconnaissance Wing, under which came the four

American squadrons at Mount Farm. His Photographic Intelligence Staff Officer was Harvey Brown.

At Medmenham, it was in the course of the reorganization before D-Day that the unit became Allied in official status as well as in fact. By this means a serious danger was averted: the possibility that its American elements might be withdrawn to form a separate unit. The direction of the Allied Central Interpretation Unit fell to Douglas Kendall, and in partnership with one of the most experienced of the Americans, Lieutenant Colonel William J. O'Connor, he steered the final stages of the work that was Medmenham's share in the preparations for the Normandy landings.

The immeasurably vast and complex undertaking of planning for the landings depended in many ways on photography. Years before the final choice of beaches was made, for instance, interpreters had been watching the whole shoreline of northern France. At different tide levels, and at different times of year, the shifting stretches of sand and mud between high and low water marks were examined. The cycle of effects caused by seasonal storms, the size and shape of underwater reefs and sandbanks, the positions of breakwaters and beach exits – all were carefully recorded, so that when the time came the planners would have the information they needed.

The work of the Army interpreters had also been a long-term project. They had been watching the coastal defences for more than three years, and constantly updating their records. They knew every gun emplacement, every pillbox, every wire entanglement, and every trench system of the whole Atlantic Wall. Another tremendous undertaking was the detailed interpretation of all radar installations along the Channel coast to a distance of twenty miles inland. This was vital to the success of the attacks which silenced enemy radar before the landings.

Preliminary models of the whole Channel coast had been made from photographs as early as 1942. But for the actual D-Day briefings 340 models were mass-produced in synthetic rubber. Models were also made of typical waves that might be expected on the beaches, based on photographic data as to the beach gradients, and statistics on the tides and currents. In addition to the models, astronomical quantities of photographs were needed for the briefings, and at this time Medmenham's photographic section was turning out something like seven million prints a month.

Such were only a few of the contributions to the planning for D-Day. Both the Americans and the British took part in what was a fully Allied achievement. It seems worthy of mention that Elliott Roosevelt, in his book *As He Saw It* (which is for the most part painfully anti-British), pays the following tribute to his RAF colleagues:

> In view of the criticisms which I have expressed in regard to some of the British warmakers, I am anxious to set it down that these RAF officers with whom I worked from mid January up until D-Day and thereafter until the final Nazi capitulation were a group of consummately knowledgeable officers, thoroughly familiar with their job and individually and severally as hard-working and as anxious to win the war as quickly as possible as any group of men it would have been possible to find. Not only were they a constant credit to their country, but they were in large part responsible for the small percentage of losses suffered in the invasion itself. I know I speak for all the American officers who worked with RAF reconnaissance experts in according them a considerable amount of the credit for the success of our arms in Europe.

It was during this time that the Americans lost one of their greatest friends. Early in 1944, for a few weeks, Adrian Warburton was at Mount Farm. By then he was a Wing Commander, with the American DFC as well as five

British decorations – DSO and bar and DFC and two bars. Even though he had been grounded, following a serious motor smash in Tunis, his presence buoyed up the Lightning pilots.

He was not supposed to fly, but on 12 April he took off in a Lightning for a flip across the Alps to San Severo. He was going to photograph some German airfields on the way out, and more targets on the way back. An American pilot who accompanied him some of the way spoke with him last near Lake Constance, and then saw him continue his southward flight alone. But Warburton never reached San Severo, and till this day his fate remains a mystery.

The sky over southern Germany was soon to become an increasingly dangerous place. On the afternoon of 25 July 1944 a Mosquito took off from Benson to photograph targets near Stuttgart and Munich. The pilot was Flight Lieutenant A.E. Wall, and Flying Officer A.S. Lobban was navigator. Late that night there was no news of them, but finally a signal came from Italy saying that Wall and Lobban had landed there – after a twenty-minute engagement with a Messerschmitt Me 262. It was the first time an Allied plane had been intercepted by a jet-propelled fighter.

By the next evening Wall was safely back in England, and on 28 July he came over to Medmenham. I listened breathlessly as he described his escape. He said that just after photographing his targets Lobban told him that a strange-looking plane was closing in on them at terrific speed. They knew it must be a jet. Many Me 262s had been photographed on the Bavarian airfields, and they had been warned that they might meet them.

Wall turned the Mosquito as sharply as he could, and the jet was going so fast that it overshot by miles, and then swung round in a huge circle to attack again. Six times the jet got into position, and six times Wall made a tight turn to evade it. Then at last over the Austrian Tyrol he escaped into cloud.

It was strange to hear his story, for my own experiences of German fighters had been quite the opposite to Wall's. For several years I had been busily engaged in pursuing *them*. Since it proved a very absorbing chase, which met with some success, I think it deserves to be described in some detail.

●　　　●　　　●

The watch that I kept for new types of aircraft, especially jets, was a separate undertaking from the watch on the aircraft factories, although the same photographs often gave news of both. But in its own way it proved to be just as valuable, for I could often describe and measure the new prototypes, so that their performance could be estimated and recognition drawings prepared, months or even years before they appeared in combat. In the last chapter I have told of my search for pilotless aircraft at Peenemünde; but keeping an eye on Peenemünde was a minor task compared to the long-term watch on the new types of the whole German aircraft industry.

It all began as early as 1941, when my section had been going only a few weeks. On a Rostock sortie I found a large aircraft which I could not identify sitting on the Heinkel airfield at Marienehe. This discovery greatly interested Michael Golovine at the Air Ministry, who at that time was badly in need of information about the new Heinkel bomber, the He 177. Form then on I knew that any reports I issued on new aircraft would be appreciated. But it was a hap-hazard business, because in those days the factory airfields were never 'laid on' as reconnaissance targets, and were photographed only occasionally by chance.

Then early in 1942 Bomber Command attacked Rostock on four consecutive nights. My special interest in the raids was that they would mean several new covers of the

Heinkel works; and after the damage assessment interpreters had finished with the photographs I pored over Marienehe at leisure. The photographs were beautifully sharp, the best 36-inch variety, and I went from building to building, not looking for anything in particular, but eager to see what had happened at the factory I knew so well. At the time of the attacks it was producing He 111s, and many half-finished bombers had been rescued from the main assembly shop. At first I lingered over the damage, which for those days was considerable, but then an apparition suddenly stopped me. Alongside the debris was a slim long-nosed aeroplane quite unlike anything I had ever seen before. Streamlined and elegant, it had the sort of high tail that means a tricycle undercarriage – an aeroplane of a new generation, which made the bombers look like limbering relics. In great excitement I showed it to Sims, and then immediately started measuring it and describing its design for Golovine.

Late that evening, as I bicycled back to my billet, I wondered whether we got that preview by a narrow margin. But actually it made no difference whether Heinkel's men put the prototype under cover five minutes after the photographs were taken or five hours. The image of the He 280, the fighter which Ernst Heinkel claims was the first twin-jet aircraft in the world to fly, was permanently on record in Medmenham's files.

Soon after this Golovine arranged for monthly meetings to discuss all the latest news on German aircraft, both from photographs and from other sources. These conferences, later nicknamed 'astrologers' meetings', were great fun and extremely helpful too. Golovine used to take charge, with a wing commander, two squadron leaders, three flight lieutenants, and myself sitting round the table, and we discussed in turn first all the fighters and rumours of fighters, and then all the bombers. The jets were of course much the most interesting thing that was coming along.

At the first meeting I explained why my reports on new types were so few and far between.

'You see, it's only by chance that the factory airfields are covered, and even then the scale is sometimes so small that you can't identify a Ju 52. The Junkers factory at Dessau has never been covered at all yet, nor the Arado or the Henschel parent factories. And of course we've never seen Rechlin. . . .' I was certain that the GAF airfield at Rechlin, where acceptance trials were flown, must be littered with new types.

'I suggest,' said Golovine, 'that you should prepare a statement on the need for regular cover, and I'll see what can be done.'

The results were beyond my wildest dreams. In the autumn of 1942 more than fifty airfields where prototypes were likely to appear were put on the flying programme for monthly cover, with emphasis on the need for good scale. This meant that during the years that followed I had a regular flow of first-class material and was able to report on a great many of the latest products of the German aircraft industry.

There was never a dull moment from then till the end of the war, what with the asymmetrical Bv 141, the twin-fuselage Heinkel glider-tug, and the last-ditch 'composite aircraft'. But they were the light relief. The main job was watching for the more orthodox types which might go into large-scale production – especially jet fighters.

Ever since I had noticed the fan-shaped marks and the long streaks on the airfield at Peenemünde, I had been on the lookout for pairs of such marks that would betray the presence of twin-jet aircraft, even if the planes themselves were out of sight. In the summer of 1943 we began to find pairs of jet marks at airfield after airfield.

I had a fortunate chance of showing these photographs to the man who was the world's greatest authority on jet propulsion, Frank Whittle. Then a Group Captain, he came to visit Medmenham with a party from the RAF

Staff College. He was enthralled by what I had found, and later, as a result of this visit, special cover of certain British airfields was flown, and I was able to compare the marks made by the British and the German jets. Group Captain Whittle stayed some time examining the pictures and giving me most valuable advice.*

I showed him my best photographs of the Me 163s at Peenemünde, and in mid 1943 tailless aircraft looked very sinister and brave-new-world; although what those Me 163s *literally* looked like, on good photographs, were little white butterflies. Later, when the Luftwaffe got them and painted them a darkish colour, they often didn't look like anything at all. In a memorandum which I wrote to try to help Second Phase interpreters I warned them that when Me 163s are not light-coloured their wings sometimes 'fade out' completely; and an Me 163 without visible means of support is the sort of thing one might well interpret as an 'object' rather than an aircraft.

My earliest report on the Me 163 went out just over a year before it first operated. But in spite of our regular cover of factory airfields and experimental stations there was still a considerable element of chance in the spotting of new types, and I did not have my first sight of an Me 262 until February 1944, only six months before it went into combat. From then on, however, we became extremely familiar with the aggressive looking little twin-jet; many hundreds of them were built before the end of the war.

I felt quite sad when I found that my first jet fighter, the He 280, had been dropped in favour of the Me 262, and

* In his book *Jet*, Sir Frank Whittle mentions that on the way back to the Staff College there was quite a lot of leg-pulling about the time he had spent with me, also some conjecture as to what my perfume was. So perhaps I should put on record that the perfume in question was Guerlain's *L'Heure bleue*, which I used rather too lavishly in those days, on the theory that the masculinity of WAAF uniform needed a little counteracting.

wondered what had gone wrong. We knew there had been a hitch because at Heinkel's branch factory outside Vienna we found airframes for He 280s parked disconsolately on the airfield and could tell from the lack of track activity that no one had been near them for weeks. But Heinkel kept on till the bitter end; so the Aircraft Section at Medmenham kept on watching him. And when Ursula Kay brought me new pictures of the Vienna factory, taken on 6 December 1944, I was fascinated to see what in plan view looked like a younger brother of the He 280. Family likenesses were coming out in the new generation. Unfortunately the photographs were not good, and the little aeroplane must have had a shiny surface for it reflected so much light that no shadows showed at all. On my desk at Medmenham it looked like a flat silhouette cut out of cotton wool. We could estimate its dimensions, however, and could report that it was photographed at the end of the runway, with 'a number of vehicles and personnel' near by, which indicated that something interesting was going on. It was the He 162, the so-called 'People's Fighter', and Ernst Heinkel, in his book *He 1000*, mentions that 6 December 1944 was the date on which the prototype made its first twenty-minute test flight.

The only two jets that really counted in the Second World War were the Me 163 and the Me 262; but these two between them, especially the latter, looked like having disastrous effects on Allied photographic reconnaissance when they began operating in the summer of 1944. Before this there was only a small margin between the performance of the British photographic planes and the best of the German fighters. Both sides were bringing in improvements all the time, but except for the short period when the Fw 190s were ahead, the British held the lead. When the jets arrived, however, all precedents went by the board. The Me 262 was more than fifty miles an hour faster than the fastest Spitfire, and the Me 163 (which although often called a jet was actually rocket-propelled) could leap upwards 'like a homesick angel', as one of the American pilots described it, and then swoop down to attack.

In theory, unarmed planes cannot operate if the enemy has fighters of better performance. But in fact the jets did not put a stop to our reconnaissance, although at first there were serious losses. The Benson pilots soon developed a special technique for evading the jets by exploiting their two main weaknesses: their enormous turning circle and their short endurance. The trick was to let the enemy fighter overtake you until it was almost within firing range and then turn sharply away to right or left. The tactics which Wall had used so successfully could not fail if you had the nerve. But the really essential thing, of course, was to see the jet in time. The Mosquito crews had the advantage here, with two pairs of eyes. The solitary Spitfire pilots had to keep turning their heads, and in the summer of 1944 there was a rising incidence of the complaint known as 'PR neck'. The Americans in their Lightnings had the worst time of all: for them the only answer was fighter escort.

All the photographic pilots had to be more than ever on the alert for 'contrails'; on guard against flying at a height where they left trails themselves, and on watch for them as the first danger signal of approaching jets. There is a story that one Spitfire pilot from Benson saw the beginning of a faint white trail above him and at once started climbing to try to get above it. He found he didn't seem to be gaining on it, and the trail didn't get any longer. Then suddenly it dawned on him that the 'trail' was the crescent moon.

The pilots from San Severo, who were doing much of the photography of southern Germany, had to reckon with the jets continuously. Captain S. Pienaar, one of the South African pilots, was the first to encounter an Me 262. On 15 August 1944 he had an even worse time than Wall. Parts of his Mosquito were shot right off, and the Messerschmitt made a total of twelve attacks. Pienaar eventually escaped into cloud, and managed somehow to limp home.

The summer of 1944 was a hectic time for Italian-based photographic reconnaissance. There were the ever-increasing demands of the Armies and the Tactical Air Forces, whose new methods of interdiction and saturation depended entirely on photographs for their speed and accuracy. At the same time, covers of distant targets in the Balkans, Czechoslovakia, and Poland, as well as in southern Germany, were wanted before and after the raids of the American strategic bombers based at Foggia. And on top of all this, much photography of southern France was needed for the Allied landings on the Riviera.

Two days after the landings, on 17 August, Karl Polifka came into his headquarters at San Severo and flopped down exhausted. It was a scorching day, and he was just back from Corsica. His pilots had been busy photographing the Frejus beaches and then the advances inland, and needless to say Polifka had been in the thick of it himself.

'That makes 170 combat missions,' he told Major Morris Esmiol, his executive officer. Then he went on: 'The French boys with the 23rd Squadron are tickled to death at the idea of going over to France,' and added thoughtfully, 'too bad about Saint-Exupéry. They've sure taken it to heart.' It had been a serious responsibility having a world-famous author as one of your pilots. Polifka's usually sunny face was clouded.

•   •   •

In the context of Allied photographic reconnaissance, Antoine de Saint-Exupéry, or 'Saint Expry' as the Americans called him, was a problematical French celebrity who insisted on flying Lightnings when he was much too old and absent-minded. But the record of Saint-Exupery's persistent devotion to photographic flying is something so unique that it must be traced from its beginning to its end aside from the main course of events.

His first taste of it had been during the winter of 1939, when Group 2–33 of the French Air Force was helping to keep watch over the Rhineland. When the German offensive came in May 1940, the Group kept numbly on with its reconnaissance during the retreat, and was struggling to operate from Orly when on 23 May Saint-Exupéry made the flight over Arras which was to be the inspiration for his most famous book.

When the remnants of the Group finally reached Algiers Saint-Exupéry was with them, and then he left the Air Force and soon afterwards went to live in New York. There he wrote *Flight to Arras*, and it was published early in 1942. Immediately it was a best-seller and 'Saint-Ex' became a literary lion. Then suddenly he heard that Group 2–23 was coming to life again. It was to be adopted by the Americans in North Africa.

At once he longed to be back with them, and he managed to get to Algiers just before Tunis fell. String-pulling was needed before he was allowed to fly Lightnings, for he was then 43 – twenty years older than most of the photographic pilots. Although he had flown more than 6,000 hours as an airline pilot, Saint-Exupéry was not in fact very good at flying Lightnings, and he admitted as much. But he was still utterly determined to keep on, and on 27 July 1943 he took off from La Marsa on his first operational sortie over southern France. After photographing his targets he was on his way back when he was drawn down as by a magnet to have a look at a little town near the coast: Agay, his sister's home. He returned in a mood of exaltation, exclaiming: 'You cannot imagine what it feels like to see one's country again!'

Only five days later, however, he was in the depths of despair. After a minor mishap (he overshot the runway at

La Marsa and finished up in a vineyard with a damaged propeller and wing) he was told that he would have to be grounded.

For eight miserable months Saint-Exupéry lived in Algiers, with no proper job and too unhappy and nervy to write. Then in the spring of 1944 his old friend General Chassin arranged to have him attached to his own bomber squadron. But Saint-Exupéry begged Chassin to get him back to photographic reconnaissance.

By this time General Eaker was in command of the Mediterranean air forces; so it was to Eaker that the two Frenchmen appealed, and the American general unwillingly agreed to allow Saint-Exupéry five more missions with his old unit. In mid-May he rejoined it joyfully, at Alghero in Sardinia, and the next two months were blissfully happy. During his time Saint-Exupéry set down some of his last impressions of photographic reconnaissance.

Once again I am experiencing the joys of high-altitude flights. They are like a diver's plunges into the depths of the sea: one enters forbidden territory, decked out in barbarous equipment, encased in a framework of dials and instruments and gauges; and high above one's country one breathes oxygen manufactured in the United States. The air of New York in the skies of France – isn't it odd? At the controls of this light, fleet monster, this Lightning P-38, there is no feeling of movement, but, rather, of being fixed and immobile at one and the same moment, over a whole continent.

The photographs one brings back are submitted to stereoscope analysis, as organisms are examined under a microscope; the interpreters of these photographs work exactly like the bacteriologists. They seek on the vulnerable body of France traces of the virus which devours her. One can die from the effects of these enemy strongholds and depots and convoys which, under the lens, appear like tiny bacilli.

And then those hours of poignant meditation as one flies over France – so near and yet so far. One feels separated from her as though by centuries. All one's tender memories and associations, indeed one's very raison-d'être, are to be found there, stretched out, as it were, 35,000 feet below, in the clear glint of the sun; and yet, more inaccessible than the treasures of the Pharaohs under the glass-cases of a museum.

By the first week of July 1944, when his unit moved to Borgo in Corsica, he had already exceeded his five flights. He was having a whole series of minor accidents and amazing escapes, and his squadron commander, who was gravely concerned about him, decided to confide to him the date of the landings, which would mean that he could no longer fly over enemy territory. But he begged for just one more flight, and as it was 'Saint-Ex' he got his way. The secret date was not mentioned. Early on 31 July he took off on that 'one more' flight – for cover of Annecy and Grenoble – the flight from which he never returned.

• • •

Throughout the final stages of the war, the vast programme of strategic photography over Europe continued from Britain and from the Mediterranean, and also from several distant outposts where for a time Allied detachments were sent (RAF Spitfires operated from a base near Murmansk, and American Lightnings from Poltava in the Ukraine). But an even vaster number of short-range reconnaissance sorties was being flown from behind the Allied lines. Both the Armies and the Tactical Air Forces that fought their way across Europe were equipped for photographic reconnaissance on a prodigious scale. Each day that weather permitted, these 'private fleets' of aircraft sped back and forth taking photographs, and the activity also continued through the lengthening autumn nights, for both the British and the Americans were making use of flashlight reconnaissance to keep track of the enemy's nocturnal movements.

And then suddenly at the end of the year came a shattering blow. On 16 December 1944 the Germans launched their offensive in the Ardennes; and during the turmoil after the break-through the question that leapt to every mind was: 'Why didn't the photographs tell us it was coming?' It was a very natural question. Rash claims had been made to the effect that photographs supplied eighty per cent of all intelligence. And with swarms of photographic planes in the European Theatre, and armies of interpreters, it seemed there must have been a bad slip-up somewhere. The atrocious winter weather had helped the enemy – that was obvious. And in many ways the Germans had been extremely careful and extremely clever, while the Allies on their side had become dangerously over-confident. But, nevertheless, there had been a serious failure of intelligence. It needed to be looked into thoroughly.

On 14 January 1945 an investigating mission with three American and three British members, including Douglas Kendall and Harvey Brown, set off for the snow-covered Western Front, and during the next fortnight they travelled 1,700 miles and visited twenty-four different units. They found that the two American Groups responsible for photography in the area of the break-through had managed, in spite of the weather, to fly 174 sorties during the first half of December; and although some of the covers were cloud-obscured, the interpreters had found and reported a considerable amount of abnormal activity. This information – the raw material of intelligence – had not, however, been converted into a form in which it could tell a coherent story.

One evening Kendall and Brown talked it all over. Kendall had very definite views.

'We've *got* to try and make people think of PR in

relation to the whole European theatre even now,' he said, 'not in relation to little bits of the front. And we must try to explain that interpretations which aren't coordinated are sometimes no more use than undeveloped films. If the Ardennes photographs had gone on to an interpretation unit that was in a position to review the whole front, I bet you the significance of what was happening would have been spotted. The "penny packet" system just doesn't work.'

'But are you sure, Douglas?' queried Brown. 'First Phase reports often have to be acted on within a few hours. I believe that each army *must* have its own set-up.'

'They didn't in Italy,' Kendall reminded him, 'and you know how well things worked there. That was a much narrower front, of course, but the same principle applies. Mind you, I don't mean for a moment that First Phase can be dispensed with, or that the commanders on the spot should be prevented from laying on what sorties they want. But there's no reason why all PR shouldn't be properly coordinated. The whole thing would be infinitely more efficient; and much more flexible and economical too.'

It was far too late in the war, however, to introduce major changes. The Mission's report, recommending that there should, at least, be a high-ranking Director of Photographic Reconnaissance responsible to the Supreme Commander, was read, and discussed, and then filed quietly away.

• • •

All through the war, those concerned with photographic intelligence had been too busy to think much about what the Germans were doing in the same line. But in the early months of 1945, as the Allied armies were closing in on Germany and elaborate plans were going ahead for ground checks of various kinds, many began to give it thought. Various questions raised themselves. Had

German technical skill led to great achievements or not? What areas in Britain and on the Eastern Front had been covered? And most important of all, where was the Germany 'library' – the record of all *they* had photographed during the war?

Before long it was established that the German library was at Zossen, just south of Berlin, and there seemed no doubt that it would fall into Russian hands. Soon, however, reports began to come through that it had been moved, but none of them said definitely where to, though one hinted that all the prints and films had been dumped in a lake near Berlin.

VE-Day came and went. By this time Harvey Brown was attached to the Supreme Headquarters in France, and there he met a WAAC Captain named Alice Davey, who had just come over to Europe. Both of them were intent on finding out as much as possible about German PI Alice Davey, who had been helping to compile interpretation manuals in the Pentagon, was wildly enthusiastic. She helped with many of the interrogations, and gradually a picture began to build up. It was a terrifying picture; a horrible warning as to what photographic intelligence can become if it is based on the wrong concepts and staffed almost entirely by uninspired plodders.

One day she came into Harvey Brown's office with a wad of pencilled notes. She had been questioning the elderly German who had been head of the interpretation school. 'He's just a poor worn out old man,' she told Harvey, 'and he hasn't a clue where the library is.' The usual story. They were both glumly thinking that perhaps they would never find the library at all when the telephone rang and Harvey answered. Suddenly he sprang to his feet, clutching the receiver as if it might get away.

'What's that? Where? Yes, of course I'll come at one.'

He rang off and for a moment was dumbfounded.

'*What* have they found?' Alice Davey was dancing with excitement. 'And *where* is it? Where?'

'Can you believe it,' said Harvey slowly. 'That was from Berchtesgaden. The man in charge of one of the joint ground-check teams. He says they've found a lot of big boxes in a barn near Bad Reichenhall – full of bundles of photographs.' He grabbed his cap. 'I'm off!'

On the following day Kendall flew out to Salzburg and joined Harvey Brown at Bad Reichenhall. In the improvised headquarters of the ground-check team there were rows upon rows of big green boxes full of photographs – the German print library. Together Kendall and Brown picked out some of the bundles at random. They were big twelve-inch square prints – the standard size for the gigantic aerial cameras the Germans used. The first sortie was cover of a port which they recognized as Southampton. Then the next bundle of prints showed unfamiliar terrain: the Eastern Front.

'The Germans took good photographs,' said Brown.

'Yes, very good. Beautifully sharp. That's what you'd expect. It seems all the more amazing that they never even got to first base with their PI'.

'D'you know what Alice Davey has definitely established now? The interpreters were *trained* to work on single prints, instead of with stereoscopes. And they hadn't a notion how to use comparative covers.'

'No!' said Kendall incredulously.

'The Germans seem to have thought that because a camera is a machine all you've got to do is improve mechanical quality,' went on Harvey. 'All the interpreters were non-commissioned, you know, except for one officer in command of each unit.'

'Old von Fritsch was right when he said that the side with the best photographic reconnaissance would win the war,' commented Kendall. 'But it seems that Hitler and his pals didn't know what "best" meant, and didn't care much anyhow. They never found out that what counts most in PI is the people who are in it. They made all the mistakes we might have made if it hadn't been for our team of individualists.'

'Did you say our *team?*'

'Yes,' replied Kendall, 'it *was* a team. A team in spite of itself.'

INDEX